MANET

PRINTED IN BELGIUM.

MANET

BY

ROBERT REY

INSPECTOR-GENERAL OF FINE ARTS AND MUSEUMS
PROFESSOR IN THE ÉCOLE DU LOUVRE

TRANSLATED FROM THE FRENCH
BY
EVELINE BYAM SHAW

WILLIAM HEINEMANN LTD.
LONDON   TORONTO

MANET

THE disconcerting originality of Edouard Manet consists quite as much in what it disdains as in what it contributes.

It might almost be called the final fruit — the swan-song as it were — of a social class which had reached its perfection and was as a consequence doomed to extinction.

The parents and family of Edouard Manet represented an order of bourgeois patricians with many excellent qualities. They were models of common sense and respectability, but hardly any ties were left to attach them to other classes of society. They had no respect for the titled aristocracy; they knew the hollowness of their pretentions and the wretchedness underlying them. They had a tolerant smile for the « naïveté » and the appalling errors of taste of the bourgeoisie, commercial, literary or administrative (such as those one meets with in the pages of Balzac from *Ursule Mirouet* to *Les Fonctionnaires* and *Les Grands Hommes de Province à Paris*). They appraised at their true value the instability and lack of culture of the proletarian worker or the peasant according to Fourrier or Proudhon. They were not deceived by the pretentions of the social « parvenus » of industry or commerce, whose presumption and whose frequently scandalous origins they clearly perceived. Their aspirations were exhausted, only their principles were left : principles of justice, of honour and of conscience. They never allowed themselves to boast of these, of course; like the honest man of classical ages, they were without pretentions to virtue. They made no concessions, even to the prestige of learning, reflecting with Pascal that too much and too little education are both equally stupefying. Every day they became more and more isolated; to every other class of society they remained aloof and reserved.

And here was this detachment suddenly expressing itself plastically in painting.

How could the public remain indifferent to this refusal to admit its claims to consideration ? It felt itself to be insulted; in fact, it was insulted. It is never by the technical or formal aspect of a work of art that the spectator is moved to the innermost fibres of his being; it is by the artist's attitude towards him which always transpires through the work. The visitor to the picture-gallery prefers anything to the humiliating indifference of a Manet, even direct provocation, which is after all in its way a sort of homage.

Edouard Manet was born at Paris, at No. 5 rue des Petits-Augustins (renamed since 1852 rue Bonaparte), on the 23rd of January, 1832. His father was Chief of Staff at the Ministry of Justice. His mother, whose maiden-name was Fournier, was the daughter of a diplomatic agent whose career was passed mostly in Sweden; Bernadotte was her godfather. Two other sons were to be born of their union. The father and the mother we know from the picture painted by their eldest son, who had become by them the object of the greatest scandal of the century. Since that 23rd January, 1832, twenty-nine years had passed over the family's united heads. The father is seated in front of a table; he wears a frock-coat and on his head a flat-topped skull-cap. His grey beard frames the lower part of his face; his look is calm, almost severe. A little behind him stands his wife, her hair dressed in the English fashion with a parting just visible under the blue-ribboned cap. She holds a work-basket filled with balls of wool of different and strongly contrasting colours. The general effect of the picture is austere and calls up memories of a silent gathering, impressions of a twilight relieved by the glow of a few warm colours, a few steady lights defining human faces and human forms.

Manet at the age of 29 exhibited this picture in the Salon of 1861. His parents were no longer living in the rue Bonaparte, but at 69, rue de Clichy. It was there that Edouard Manet began the picture; he finished it in a studio which he had just rented in the rue de Douai. Almost as soon as it was finished, he made an etching of it; and the following year, in 1862, he engraved it a second time. The picture is redolent of some secret and impassioned emotion, a sort of reverence, an inherent nobility, which reminds one, in spite of all the differences of subject and technique, of the *Peasants Repast* by Louis Le Nain.

But it was precisely the avowal of this intimate exclusiveness that contemporary spectators, themselves debarred from all sympathic participation, found so hard to accept; they wanted to force their way within the charmed circle. The *Moniteur Universel,* through the pen of its critic, Léon Legrange, expresses very well this feeling of vexation : « M. et Mme M... must have cursed over and over again the day which put a brush into the hands of this unfeeling portrait-painter ».

Let us return to that day.

In 1840, the young Manet at the age of seven was placed as a half-boarder in an institution at Vaugirard where he remained for three years. At ten years old, he entered the college in the rue des Postes, then called Rollin College. He was an inattentive pupil. His closest confident was his uncle Fournier, a brother of his mother's, an officer of artillery. Uncle Fournier always carried a pocket-album about with him in which he used to draw at every opportunity. He was following in this a tradition already ancient among officers of the engineers and the artillery; drawing, with the survey of emplacements, siege-works and enemy positions as its object played an important part in their military education; to draw up a list of their works, in which they evidently took great pleasure, from the beginning of the XVIIth century, would be a lengthy but an extremely interesting task. Uncle Fournier unbent towards his nephew and gave him a portfolio of lithographs entitled, as one would expect : « Etudes par Charlet » (Studies by Charlet). And the child scribbled happily in the margins. At the college there was a drawing-class; the little boy had himself entered for it, in spite of the remonstrances of his father. In it he found a confident, a pupil like himself, called Antonin Proust, destined for a high administrative post. Together with Uncle Fournier, who took them to the Louvre on Sunday, the three formed a band of conspirators. Very soon other studies were so neglected for the sake of drawing, that the director of the college, M. de Faucompret, thought fit to report to the elder M. Manet.

The usual struggle between experience and genius was to open once more. Sentence was passed : Edouard Manet was to abandon his day dreams and study law. He refused. As a concession, they gave him a choice : law or the navy. He chose the navy, went up for the examination at the Naval College, and failed. He had reached the age-limit; the entrance examination was closed to him, unless he took advantage of a « spell at sea » before presenting himself again. On December 9, 1848, the transport ship *Havre de Guadeloupe,* with Captain Besson in command, was being fitted out for Rio. The young Edouard Manet, aged sixteen, signed on as a pilot's apprentice. Seven months later he was back once more. His father had thought things over in the meantime. He gave way; it was the best thing he could have done. At the beginning of the year 1850, Edouard Manet, who was just eighteen, entered the studio of Thomas Couture, where he was soon joined by Antonin Proust, his old ally.

There followed a long period of six years during which the various elements of his highly-strung and fragile temperament were to establish themselves. It was an adolescent boy of eightteen who entered the studio of Couture; it was an adult man of twentyfour who left it in 1856, slamming the door behind him. If a romance was to be made of this life, it would have to be entitled : « Manet, or intelligence ». He possessed in an extreme degree a sense of the ridiculous and of the vulgar. He must have felt from the first that he was making a mistake in entering the studio of Couture, that admirably clever and gifted rogue, so simple and at the same time so crafty, so absurdly infatuated with his own self-importance. For a rogue he was, an over-blown flower of that race of rogues who were among the most noxious weeds of the XIXth century, and whose artificial turbulence concealed an old-fashioned respect for academic awards and medals. Couture borrowed from everyone; his incontestable virtuosity, his horse-coper's instincts, stood him in good stead.

From every one of the geniuses of his time he took some inflexion; an excellent workman, he watered the wine of others, diluted it, seasoned it with a spice of conservative morality and intoxicated with this mediocre liquor a public as stupid as any in our history.

In this studio, Edouard Manet preserved a demeanour of detachment even in his affability, with an ironic smile at the corners of his lips so fine and so keen-edged that from the first the rogue submitted to his power. Couture was well aware that he had introduced a dangerous thoroughbred animal into his fold of sheep disguised as wolves. The master's aversion to his pupil (which was reciprocated) though at first more or less disguised, dated from the first day. Edouard Manet was there to gain technical proficiency, not an æsthetic standpoint. When the studio closed, he continued his studies at the Swiss Academy; each week he passed long hours at the Louvre. Passionately he longed to acquire the whole grammar of the art of drawing. Alas! from that moment he was doomed; he was too intelligent. He grasped too easily and too thoroughly the meaning of the works he studied, so that it did not take him long to dismantle their technique in order to discover their deeper secrets; it is to quick wits like his that such secrets are revealed.

His sketch-books are filled with innumerable drawings. He was continually making copies, as for instance, the « Virgin with a white rabbit » (*La Vierge au lapin blanc*), in the Louvre, which he signed *M. d'après T.* (Manet after Titian), and which belonged to M. Denis Cochin, the interpretation of « Jupiter and Antiope », also after Titian, and the « Little horsemen » (*Petits cavaliers*), long attributed to Velasquez, of which he made copies not only in oils but also in watercolours. He obtained from Delacroix permission to copy the *Barque du Dante* (Dante's Barque), then in the Luxembourg, and made two studies from it.

At the age of twenty he was already in serious trouble. About 1848, a young Dutch woman, Suzanne Leenhoff, a pianist, two years older than the painter, had become intimate with the Manet family. The secret passion of Suzanne Leenhoff and Edouard Manet resulted in the birth of a son on January 29, 1852. He was registered under an assumed name : Léon-Edouard Koëlla; everyone of Manet's acquaintance believed, or pretended to believe, that the child was the infant brother of Suzanne Leenhoff.

Provided with funds by his relatives, Manet went abroad on several occasions; he visited Holland, Germany, Italy; he even went as far as Prague and Vienna. At Florence he copied the head of a young man by Filippino Lippi, and the *Venus of Urbino,* after Titian. These and numerous other works are far from being his only museum studies. From each of his travels, the young man in his role of an observer of life as it is returned more confirmed in his disdain for academic effects. This accounted for the ill-humour of Couture, so often evoked : « You will only be the Daumier of painting, and nothing more ». It also accounted, as a further consequence, in the Spring of 1856, for his departure from a studio in which he had learnt more good and more evil than he himself knew.

These results soon became evident in the twenty-four year old Edouard Manet. He was commissioned at about this time to paint a self-portrait.

We see him with quantities of hair, a fair full beard, trimmed rather short, surrounding his chin and partly covering his cheeks; a grey cravat is folded at his neck, the jacket is grey and the waistcoat black. Perhaps Manet executed this commission, signed *Un ami. Ed Manet* (A friend. Ed. Manet) for Antonin Proust, in whose possession for a long time it was. With Albert de Balleroy, a painter of hunting subjects, he rented a studio in the rue Lavoisier.

The half-length figure of « Christ with the Palm » (*Christ au Roseau*) whose first owner was Edouard Manet's childhood's friend, the Abbé Hurel, is no doubt to be dated from these first days of emancipation. The studio in the rue Lavoisier became in a few months the meeting-place of young painters with independent views. At the Salon of 1859 Manet was to come into contact with the great public for the first time. Meanwhile, between this Spring of 1856 and then, it was in this studio that he accumulated various studies and trial-pieces, such as the « Boy with the cherries » (*Le gamin aux cerises*). The model for this, a poor boy of hypochondriac tendencies, was found one morning hanged in the studio. He was the same model who had already sat for the « Boy with the red cap » (*Le gamin à la toque rouge*). Other works done at this time include the « Child with a sheep » (*L'enfant au mouton*), a little naked shepherd boy in a landscape, clasping a lamb in his arms; the « Woman with the Dogs » (*La femme aux chiens*), the « Woman with a pitcher » (*La femme à la cruche*), and the portrait of the Abbé Hurel. Finally, there is the « Absinthe drinker » (*Le buveur d'absinthe*), to-day in the Ny Carlsberg Museum at Copenhagen. This work, which the jury of the Salon of 1869 were to reject unreservedly, was the result of long meditation. Manet had not entirely broken with Couture, but there was a marked absence of cordiality in their relationship; in painting the « Absinthe drinker », Manet hoped to put his former master out of countenance. He had to pose for him a certain Collardet who had gone down in the world, but in whose habitual drunkenness there was preserved a certain air of distinction. He showed him leaning against a wall, the base of which forms a narrow seat or ledge on which the drinker has stood his glass half-full of the beautiful opalescent but poisonous liquid. The bottle like a sort of long-necked bomb, black save for a small white reflection on its shiny surface, has rolled to the ground. The man has a romantic cape draped round him, rather dramatically; a large top hat, very high, very curved, sinks down almost over his eyes; between the hat which conceals it from above and the beard which covers the cheeks appears the face, brutal and weak; it is lighted on one side only. The cape envelops the body down to the knees. The drinker stands with his weight thrown on to his right leg, whilst the left, stiffened in front and touching the ground with the tip of the toe, seems to sketch an involuntary dance movement. Certainly there was novelty in this use of the medium thickly applied and enclosed within contours traced with the brush in brown; there was novelty in the use of these blacks, sooty but at the same time luminous. But even these effects, it was felt — it will long be felt — were derived from Couture himself. Manet owed this way of modelling faces by means of contrasted light, the silhouetted effect of these opaque shadows, to him. But unlike his master, he disdained to make a coquettish use of them. He exaggerated them, on the other hand, obtaining effects of a tragic intensity, like Daumier, in fact. And Couture would not have been far wrong if he had suppressed from his prophecy the « nothing more » and the bitterness. Couture, who was invited to see the picture in the rue Lavoisier, before it was sent to the Salon, treated it contemptuously as madness and its painter as a « drunkard yourself ». The break was final. Some days later, the picture was refused by the jury, as might have been expected.

After this first passage at arms, the name of Manet began to circulate in the studios, sometimes as that of a victim, sometimes as that of a madman. At this time, the Martinet Gallery in the boulevard des Italiens opened, and here the man in the street was confronted with some of these works, the sentiment of which was so new. The age of scandal had begun.

The « Absinthe drinker » exhibits a certain awkwardness, or rather, a certain stiffness and tension, a slight strain. Manet was to relax more successfully in another work, far more profoundly original, which he painted in 1860 : « Music in the gardens of the Tuileries » (*La musique aux Tuileries*) (London, National Gallery). The whole picture is an effect of free observation. The elements of the composition, trees, foliage and people, are conceived of as coloured volumes, not merely as the vehicles of their local colours; in fact as radiating centres of colours and shapes, by the mere force of their being in movement independently or in relation to each other. No picture of the XIXth century, except perhaps certain of the sketches of Carpeaux, furnishes such an example of the dynamic quality of Nature. In none had the intensification of certain colours by shadow been so emphatically declared; above all, in none is the attempt to recover on canvas the complete and fugitive vision of a moment stated in so unique a manner, so entirely freed from any literary or intellectual overtones. We know that this silhouette represents Albert de Balleroy, and that one Manet himself; Zacharie Astruc and Mme Lejosne, whose husband, an officer, was a friend of Baudelaire, Théophile Gautier, Champfleury, Fantin-Latour, Aurélien Scholl, the painter Monginot, also appear in the picture. Did they all pose? Presumably they did not. Did any of them even pose? Manet gives the forms the contours memory suggested. He uses them, and no more. There is no connexion between a work of this sort and the « Conversation pieces » which Fantin was at this time meditating; but there are many connexions, for example, with *Le Moulin de la Galette,* in which Renoir, some fifteen years later, was to make use of his friends, without a thought of recording the details of their iconography for posterity. This picture remained for three years in the studio. Edouard Manet had undertaken the portrait of his father and mother of which we spoke at the beginning of this essay. At the same time he was experimenting with etching, and making water-colours and often reverted to earlier *motifs* in one or other of these mediums.

One of the last pictures of the year 1860 was no doubt the « Spanish singer » (*Chanteur espagnol*). This was the first fruits of that infatuation for everything Spanish which became with Manet an obsession soon after the time when the guitarist Huerta (composer of the hymn to Riego) was all the rage in Paris. Seated on a bench, his guitar pressed against the hollow of his stomach, he is singing. A rose-coloured silk scarf as a head-band, under the broad-brimmed black felt hat, detaches itself curiously from a brick-red and burnt umber background in the style of Van Dyck. The visit to Paris of a troupe of singers and dancers had aroused in Manet an ardent curiosity. The types and costumes gave him exactly the sort of colour he had been wanting.

This time the jury's verdict was favourable. Not only was the « Spanish singer » admitted, but it was awarded an honourable mention. Théophile Gautier, in his guide to the Salon of 1861, treats it to a truculent description. The good Théo found in it matter for literature and he asked nothing better of a painting. His feeling for plastic form was, after all, almost non-existent; Corot and Millet knew that fact already, and Edouard Manet was soon to have an opportunity of discovering it too.

It was at this time that Manet left the rue de Douai and took a new studio in the rue Guyot, which was to be his abode until 1871. His enthusiasm for everything Spanish did not prevent him from sometimes painting views in the suburbs of Paris, such as the big picture « Fishing » (*La Pêche*) in which appear Suzanne Leenhoff (soon to become Mme Edouard Manet) and the little Koëlla. But he reverted constantly to Spanish subjects. He even went as far as to make use once more of the « Little horsemen » to compose a painting of a sort of studio of the time of Philip IV, in which one sees Velasquez at work surrounded by noblemen; in another picture a child (Léon Koëlla) brings a tray to the same noblemen. When he interrupts these evocations of the past, it is to undertake a study of the nude for which Suzanne Leenhoff is the model. But Spain immediately recalls him. Here again is the young Koëlla; he holds in his arms a heavy sword, the belt of which dangles against his legs (New York, Metropolitan Museum). Manet made two etchings of this subject. Carried away by the taste for *picaresque* themes, he assembles in a frieze on a large canvas nearly three metres in length, not only his « Absinthe drinker » and an old Jewish strolling violonist, but also a beggar, of the name of Gueroult, a turbanned Saracen, two little boys and a little gypsy girl carrying a small child. This curious work, known by the name of the « Old musician (*Vieux musicien*), is not without affinity, at least in its mysterious atmosphere and its disjointedness, with Courbet's famous « studio ». Of the « Old musician » he was not long in making a more attractive version : the « Street singer ». This time the model was a young woman, Victorine Meurend who, during the next twelve years, was often to pose for Manet. A desultory performer on the guitar and at times a model as circumstances required, with her arched brows, her finely drawn and rather angular contours, the subdued delicacy of her colouring, she was for Manet the support he needed for constructing his figures, so impassive and aloof. She was to end her career with the painful renunciation of the rather foolish dreams and artistic pretentions which came to her later on. But at that time she still had her freshness intact, its integrity as yet unsullied.

In works like the « Boy with the sword » (*L'Enfant à l'épée*) and the « Street singer » (*Chanteuse des rues*), Manet affirms his taste, already avowed, for the faces of sleep walkers who stare at you with open but unseeing eyes, pursuing who knows what dream behind the crystal clear and limpid but impenetrable black of their gaze. This way of discountenancing while at the same time ignoring the public was the most disconcerting insolence that could have been perpetrated at the time; Manet seldom failed in it. But he could not long remain silent about Spain. Here is a « Gypsy girl with a cigarette » (*Gitane à la cigarette*). Then, as an overdoor decoration, a still-life with a guitar and a sombrero; then again a group of Spanish dancers among whom is a seated dancer, the first appearance of « Lola of Valencia ». The models formed part of a troop led by the dancer Mariano Campruni, who was enjoying a triumph at the Hippodrome. Almost as soon as he had painted this group, Manet undertook the full-length portrait of Lola, half life-size. The quatrain of Baudelaire written on this dancer, her black mantilla draped across her bust, in the full-skirted dress trimmed with *pompoms*, which he compared to a rose and black jewel, is well-known. We also know that the Judges very perversely condemned it as immoral on this account. This work is among the most celebrated of Manet's pictures. Is it one of the best? I think not. Certain demands must be made of genius; the genius of Manet can stand the test. « Lola of Valencia » is a *résumé* of his failings. The face is drawn by means of large brown scar-like marks which do not succeed at all well in giving the impression of modelling or depth. The right arm is without substance, the left leg is slurred over in a half-shadow, the figure poses lifelessly on one foot; the red woollen *pompoms* which ornament the dress are no more than patches of colour. All the brown sauce absorbed by Manet in the studio of Couture emerges here. Alas! there was still some more of it to be got out of his system. The few very tasteful passages of painting that are nevertheless to be found in this picture, — for example, the painting of the right leg in its tight sheath of coarse pink silk, — are discords which serve rather to detract from the general effect than to enhance it. In fact, we feel irritated with Manet who was able, not to content us, but to content himself with so little. The « amateur » character of his painting, and the ease with which he could stop sometimes with his intention only half fulfilled is in evidence here. It is for this reason that this picture shows at what point Manet may become a dangerous example to the young. But in fact, apart from Chardin and Cézanne, how many masters can one think of whose every brush-stroke or chalk-mark is exemplary in every one of their works? Besides, Lola has been unfortunate. To-day she is in the Camondo collection in the Louvre, hanging close by those two impeccable touchstones : *Le modèle à l'atelier* («The model») of Corot and the little sketch of the *Joueurs de cartes* (« Cardplayers ») of Cézanne; she is ill at ease in their company.

In this same year, 1862, Edouard Manet painted the portrait of his youngest brother, Eugène, in the costume of a Majo; that of Victorine Meurend in the costume of an Espada (both in the Metropolitan Museum); that of a young woman reclining in Spanish costume; that of Jeanne Duval, the mistress of Baudelaire (Budapest Museum), seated, emaciated and swarthy, in an immense crinoline; also several family portraits; some still-life pictures; some watercolours; and finally he had on his easel his *Déjeuner sur l'herbe* (« Picnic »).

The famous year 1863, during which the name of Edouard Manet was to spread throughout the artistic world, was approaching. Since the summer of 1862, Manet had been preparing this work. He had made innumerable studies for the landscape background in the neighbourhood of Gennevilliers. His models were Victorine Meurend, Eugène Manet, Ferdinand Leenhoff, a Dutch sculptor, the brother of Suzanne Leenhoff. In secret, Manet constructed his composition on a Raphaelesque model : « The Judgment of Paris ». The work was finished, he dated it 1863 and sent it in to the Salon, along with the young man in the costume of the Majo and the portrait of Victorine Meurend as an Espada. All three were rejected. The exclusions were so numerous, moreover, that the protestations of the victims even reached the ears of Napoleon III. It was the occasion for one of those unconventional actions on the part of the Emperor which, like some other episodes in his strange career, reveal him as a far more sympathetic character than is usually supposed. He brought about a veritable *coup d'état*. He himself would see the rejected works; with his own hand he would touch them; and by his express command, the obstructions and the ill-will of the officials were swept aside; the *Salon des Refusés* was opened, in the Palais de l'Industrie, next door to the *Salon des Admis,* or rather I ought really to say they actually opened into each other. The Emperor, accompanied by the Empress, came to see them.

There were there, besides Manet, works by Whistler, Jongkind, Fantin-Latour, Pissarro, Cazin, the etcher Bracquemond, and the sculptor Henri Cros; one also saw there pictures signed by J.-J. Laurens, Harpignies, Chintreuil, Legros, Vollon. The public is by instinct academic; it loves to jeer at the condemned. Some authors however, from that moment, faced the mob : Fernand Desnoyers, Théophile Thoré (Thoré-Burger), Edouard Lockroy, finally Zola, who praised Manet for having « realised the dream dear to all painters : to put natural figures in a landscape ». He sang the praises of this composition « so vast, so full of air... »

The crowd, which loves formulas, talked a lot about *pleinairisme;* but of course they talked at cross purposes. The *Déjeuner sur l'herbe* is not an open-air picture like some of Corot's studies, but on the contrary, a studio picture like the *Concert champêtre* by Giorgione. Even its technique was not without precedent. Why was it so outrageously shocking to the eye and to customary opinions?

Simply because the passages from full illumination to complete shadow instead of being rendered by scientific gradations of tone, starting far from the points of contrast, were defined by an abrupt transition, which accounts for the rather crude and broken effect, the stereoscopic superposition of forms silhouetted one in front of another. Courbet, with his convention of very rounded modelling — « always the same three billiard balls », as Manet said later — was still further from nature and in fact he remained faithful to the tradition of painting like a sculptor by accentuating the contour to the limits of improbability. Courbet had inherited this tradition from the followers of David to whom he was directly connected through his first masters. Whilst Manet, by adhering to a scarcely perceptible modelling of bodies and faces, rediscovered on his own account the intense verisimilitude of certain of the portraits of Holbein. But Holbein had been forgotten for so long that to revive him amounted to creating in every picture a startling novelty. While the uproar was at its height among the critics and in the studios, Manet (who, during the course of a short journey to Holland, had just effected his union with Suzanne Leenhoff) was beginning the masterly piece of work known as *L'Olympia* (« Olympia »).

It was the portrait of Victorine Meurend lying on a bed, attired in a pearl and a gold bracelet. Her left hand rests on her right thigh, the gesture of the large nymph reclining in the foreground of Poussin's *Triomphe de Flore* (« Triumph of Flora ») in the Louvre. In the background on the right a negress, wearing a cotton print dress, brings her mistress a bouquet. At the foot of the bed, a black cat arches its back.

There again Manet could have quoted his authorities; he would have found them among the works of Titian and Goya. There again the difference of treatment between the technique of this work and that of generally accepted works of art was almost negligible; but this almost negligible difference was enough to bewilder, even to terrify, the visitors to the Salon of 1863. None of the weaknesses which are so detrimental to « Lola of Valencia » are present in « Olympia ». The colours, which in that picture were still lacking in refinement, are here of an infinite delicacy; in the folds of the sheet alone the harmony of the grey tones is without equal. Manet seems to have forced the shadows defining the contours to recede so as to compress themselves within the limits of the outline. There in fact, they are, within an incredibly narrow space, but miraculously shaded off, so well indeed that the form takes its full volume without losing any of its natural clarity.

Since Cranach's pictures of Venus, no nude body had ever been depicted quite so naked, so truly divested of all the marks with which, for four hundred years, the imitation in painting of sculptured volumes had set it off. A custom of such long standing is not abolished in a day. To read plastic works implies a deciphering. This deciphering process even among children is as spontaneous as the use of their mother tongue, but only on condition that the practice is ancestral and of common usage. And as the actual realism of Manet used, if the metaphor may be permitted, a forgotten alphabet, the public, confronted by « Olympia », remained gaping. Certainly it perceived, in spite of itself, the intense reality of this nude; it found itself in the presence no longer of an ideographic theme but of a human body without a chemise.

I remember my first encounter, forty years ago, with « Olympia », and the strangely painful shock which I received. I was afraid when I saw the pallid form, the small face with the skin stretched as though over wood. « Olympia » frightened me like a corpse, and yet I felt oppressed by the malevolence of her gaze, so terribly alive. Is it necessary to recall the indignant clamour which was aroused? In almost all the contemporary criticisms is found the same horror at this nudity, too realistic in colour, in whose presence was evoked only the thought of the unclothed bodies which could be seen in the dissecting room.

« The crowd throngs in front of M. Manet's putrefying Olympia as though at the Morgue » (Paul de Saint-Victor, *La Presse,* 28 May, 1865). « The flesh tones are dirty, the modelling non-existent » (Théophile Gautier, *Moniteur Universel,* 24 June). « This red-haired brunette is of a studied ugliness; her face is stupid, her skin cadaverous... All this chaotic disparity of colours, of impossible forms, arrests our gaze and stupefies us » (Félix Deriège, *Le Siècle,* 2 June), etc., etc.

Manet, it is true, was unable then to foresee what a warcry his work was to become; the subscription, started seven years after his death, to acquire and offer it to the State; the hesitations of his childhood's friend, Antonin Proust, then Minister of Fine Arts; at last the transference of « Olympia » to the Louvre in November 1907 (forty two years after) by order of Clemenceau, who thus fulfilled a prophecy of Zola's.

Of course the scandalised majority were opposed by the enthusiastic minority.

Manet could have said with Vauvenargues : « It is not a great misfortune not to succeed with all sorts of people ». Quite a group of defenders was found to support him with zealous passion. There was Zacharie Astruc whose poetic inspiration had already been given free rein in connection with « Lola of Valencia »; Baudelaire; the astonishing M. Chocquet, employed at the Ministry of Finance; Zola (who was about to inaugurate in *L'Evénement* such an active campaign in favour of Manet that the indignant readers obliged Villemessant, the Director of *L'Evénement,* to part with his critic (which he did); the liberal leader writer Théodore Duret, and many others.

Soon their general headquarters became the famous Café Guerbois, 9, avenue de Clichy, which was until 1875 the meeting place of so-called independent painters and writers. Manet, with his air of distinction, and his vivacious wit, set off, to give it a final polish, by a suspicion of the dandy, was its most brilliant frequenter. In spite of his apparent ease of manner, his production was enormous. He painted innumerable studies of flowers, race-course scenes, water-colours, portraits; he also painted contemporary events such as, for example, the naval battle which took place on June 19, 1864, off Cherbourg, between the corvette « Kearsage » of the federal party and the battleship « Alabama » of the southern party. He detested the anecdote in painting, and seems to have wanted to show in this work that the dramatic element of an action is a subjective phenomenon and is not in the least spectacular. Who seeing a few boats filled by tourists in top-hats intent on the horizon where the silhouettes of two cargo-boats are surrounded by puffs of smoke like cotton-wool would believe that a murderous battle was in progress?

In 1867, when he treated in four different versions the execution of the Emperor Maximilian — at which the whole of Europe was shuddering — he gave only the humblest place to the outlines of the victim who sinks down and is hardly seen through the smoke of the firing-platoon. On the other hand, by throwing the emphasis on the rounded backs of the soldiers still taking aim at him, on their broad white belts, and on the calm bearing of the non-commissioned officer who loads his weapon for the *coup de grace,* he deliberately reduces the aspect of this tragic moment to that of some firing exercise on the parade ground.

In fact, whether he is dealing with a portrait or with an incident of great dramatic intensity, Manet preserves the same attitude to his public : he puts the facts before them but disdainfully refuses to confide to them the emotion that he feels.

In the year 1865 he painted « Angelina » (Musée du Luxembourg), « The Spaniard with the black cross » (*L'Espagnole à la croix noire*), « Christ mocked by the soldiers » (*Jésus insulté par les soldats*), for which picture Manet had to pose for him a man called Janvier, a locksmith by profession, thus reverting to the tradition of the mediæval painters and of the Spaniards of the XVIIth century who deliberately chose their models among the artisans of the street. And in this same year he was to paint, like Velazquez and Ribera, genuine cripples christened by him philosophers. At the end of the year 1865, Manet is quite definitely Manet.

The words of Pascal still apply : « It is the fight that we love and not the victory... We look not for things, but for the pursuit of things ». But from this time onwards we may consider the problem of Manet as solved.

His works may flow from his palette on a precipitate rhythm, but they have no more surprises for us. « The woman with the parrot » (*La femme au perroquet*), the « Guitar-player » (*Joueuse de guitare*), « Matador saluting » *(Un matador saluant)*, the whole of his bullfight series show him to us only more confirmed in his point of view and in the free use of his instinctive virtuosity. It may be remarked that this is the end of his fervour for Spanish subjects. During the course of a journey to Spain accomplished in 1865, he tired of his Spanish mania.

The great work of the year 1866 is the « The Fifer » (*L'Enfant de troupe jouant du fifre*) (Camondo collection); probably Victorine Meurend posed for this picture. It is an evidence of Manet's marvellous progress. The picture is composed in three stages with a sureness and readiness of hand surpassed by none. Whilst in Couture's studio they had taught him to do the whole of the underpainting of a composition in « brown sauce », but Manet refuses to allow himself such margins.

14

He places his colours directly on the canvas which is freshly prepared with an even layer of paint. His modelling into light and his modelling into shadow is achieved with the greatest economy of means. The passages from light to shadow are still narrower and more scientific in their incredible abruptness than formerly when he was painting « Olympia ». To the face and the flesh-tones he gives an extraordinarily vivid surface by means of first laying them in in a medium light tone, then indicating the shadows and, as the third stage, finally adding the high lights on those parts of the picture which appear to project. He never takes any trouble to conceal his alterations, simply covering them with a broad layer of transparent colour beneath which the tone thus hidden still shines through with the happiest of effects. He mixes his colours very little. Seen from close to the red trousers seem to have the uniformity of lacquer; but some slight films of black, scarcely visible to the eye at close quarters suffice, if one stands slightly back, to model the heavy military cloth extraordinarily well. This work is placed close beside Corot's little model and Cézanne's *Joueurs de cartes*. But this time it holds its own.

Is this to say that Manet had no weaknesses? No. We know that at each instant, in his minor works, at least, the man's mind works too fast for his hand and that this annoys him. Many of his still-life paintings of flowers are of a directness that is too summary and are lacking in refinement. The little portrait of Mme Manet at the piano is at the same time exquisite and deplorable. The charming silhouette of the pianist, seen in profile, seated at her piano, detaches itself from a very inadequately modulated grey background; the beadings of the panelling are indicated too heavily and too rigidly, which makes them seem nearer than the sitter herself; the wood of the piano is of a thick tone, monotonous and without transparency. As ill luck would have it, precisely this little sketch has to make a pendant to Cézanne's sketch of the *Joueurs de cartes,* the handling of the pigment of which shows up the unevenness of Manet.

The year 1867 was the year of the Great Exhibition. Edouard Manet was to do as Courbet had done in 1865 and as Courbet did again this time. He was to put up a building at his own expense in which to exhibit most of the works of which we have been speaking. In this building his usual detractors and his faithful admirers were brought face to face. In the press, however, Manet had only one true defender : Zola. The following year, wishing to pay his debt of recognition to this faithful friend, he painted the portrait to be seen at the Louvre. Soon afterwards appeared in *Le Balcon* (« The Balcony ») the silhouette of Berthe Morisot, whose family were connected with the Manets and who was to become one of his favourite sitters.

In the Salon of 1870, he showed a large portrait : « A young woman seated in front of an easel, painting » (*Une jeune femme devant un chevalet et peignant*). The sitter was Eva Gonzalès, Manet's only pupil (she had declared a passionate admiration for her master and ended her life in 1883 some days after the death of Manet).

During the siege of Paris, Manet, aged thirty nine, was one of the artillerymen of the National Guard. By a somewhat ironic coincidence, he found himself under orders from Meissonnier! He accepted events with serenity. In one letter to his relations, he entreats them to be patient and reassures them... « I shall be at the Saint-Ouen Gate, and I shall do very well there » (November, 7, 1870)... « Take care of your health. Do not be alarmed. Patience. We have plenty of it here. I think of you ceaselessly ». In a letter dated January 30, 1871, he wrote to his wife who was at Oloron with Manet's mother and with the young Léon Koëlla : « It is all over and we are all three (himself and his two brothers) alive and whole ».

At the beginning of February he left Paris. He painted several views of the port of Arcachon and back again in Paris he resumed his strenuous life once more.

In 1873 one might have thought that a reconciliation was to take place between the public, official art and Manet. He exhibited in the Salon *Le bon bock* (« The Mug of Beer »), Philadelphia, Carroll Tyson collection. The sitter was the engraver Bellot, smoking his pipe, seated facing the spectator near a table on which stands a large *bock,* or mug of beer; the generous proportions of his stomach comfortably surmount his thighs. Unanimous praise suddenly succeeded to invectives. It is necessary perhaps to go back to the appearance in the Salon of 1824 of the *Vœu de Louis XIII* (« Vow of Louis XIII ») by Ingres to find such a revision of public opinion.

15

With his temperament, Manet found this sudden popularity disquieting. And he hastened to disenchant the public, for whose good opinion he really cared very little.

His palette was to undergo a very pronounced change. In 1874, a group of painters, called to-day the Impressionists : Claude Monet, Pissarro, Cézanne, Sisley, Renoir and some others held, as is well known, their first collective exhibition. Most of them were very much younger than Manet. (Pissarro, however, born in 1830, was his elder by two years). Through the tolerance of the jury under the Emperor, from 1863 to 1870, some of them had gained access to the Salon. But since the Commune, all painting that was not academic was held as « communal » and subject to arrest. These men had been obliged, in spite of themselves, to live in retreat for four years, alone with nature. They had freed themselves from the influences to which they had previously submitted and which were apparent in their earlier works. They used a very light palette; they painted Nature in her most impromptu aspects; they were inspired by the example of Manet. But it is certain that they in their turn had an influence on Manet. His palette lightened considerably. The deep colours and frequent use of black which had been usual with him up till then were to be exchanged for new lightness and transparence of colour. He relinquishes none of the originality of his vision, nothing of his haughty impassivity. Neither does he impose on himself any rules.

His picture of *Le linge* (« Washing day »), unanimously refused by the Salon of 1876, except for two votes (those of Bonnat and of Henner!) was exhibited in the studio he then occupied, 4, rue Saint-Pétersbourg. All the press received invitations. There was a commotion and the chorus of imprecations was no less violent than in the early days. Manet was not a man to make concessions. All the time he was producing works infinitely precious in quality, like the portrait of Stéphane Mallarmé which, of all his small portraits, may be considered as his most astonishing success (Musée du Louvre). The portraits of small dimensions alternate with large portraits like the « Nana » dressing in her *loge,* which no doubt furnished Zola with the title for his novel; the portrait of the baritone Faure in the role of Hamlet; the portrait of M. et Mme Jules Guillemet in the Conservatory (Berlin, National collection); *Le père Lathuile* (Belgium, Tournai Museum).

In considering the number of works of all sorts which he produced each year, one is astounded by the certainty of his art, by his incredible faculty for continual fresh creation. From the *Chez le père Lathuile* (« At père Lathuile's »), all the studies for which had been made out of doors, to the *Bar des Folies-Bergère* (« Bar at the Folies-Bergère ») (London, National Gallery), of the Salon of 1882, for which all the studies had been made actually at the Folies-Bergère, in the most artificial conditions of lighting, all of them present an aspect of truth so direct and so new, that one is positively astounded.

The other picture sent in to the Salon of 1882 was fairly generally well received. It was *Jeanne,* the portrait of a young girl who was to have quite an enviable theatrical career under the name of Mlle Demarcy.

From the year 1880, Manet began to feel the first attacks of the disease which was to prove fatal to him. This disease was the result of the fatigue and the too intense concentration demanded by his work; and also of the excessive strain on his temperament, naturally calm and sunny, which for more than twenty years had been subjected to a life of harassing struggle against the incomprehension, the malice, and the frivolity of a public which he would like to have dominated. It began with short attacks of rheumatism which soon became more and more frequent and more and more painful. He painted especially portraits which obliged him to stand less in front of his easel. During the summer of the year 1880 he went for a change and rest to Bellevue. The subjects of his pictures were chiefly flowers, pictures of still-life, small rustic scenes executed with a brilliance and a transparence of tone of which one can never tire. In the Salon he was represented by a large portrait of the friend of his childhood, Antonin Proust.

In 1881, although his illness was becoming worse, he still found means of executing the portrait of Rochefort, which was to appear in the Salon, and the vast picture known by the name of *M. Perthuiset,* one of the most imaginative, and surprising, of Manet's works, and one of the lightest too. Perthuiset, who enjoyed a momentary fame on account of the number of lions he had slaughtered on African soil, preserves, at the instant when the public would like to have had him tense with emotion lying in ambush for his prey, that impenetrable calm invariably held by Manet like a pane of glass between the souls of the sitter and the spectator. In producing this picture, he was able to enjoy the private satisfaction of losing none of his enemies. However, it was thanks to some very unexpected votes that the work was able to pass through the doors of the Salon. Cabanel, who presided over the jury, had dared to exclaim : « Sirs, there are not perhaps four among us who could paint a head like that ». The decision was carried by seventeen votes.

It was learnt, on June 24, 1881, after the announcement of the awards, that Manet had received a second medal. The news was received amid oaths and hisses. Manet was not among those who make partisans. And some writers, from whom one might have expected a more comprehending attitude, Huysmans, for example, abused the work as though he had been a mere Albert Wolff. « Monsieur Manet has been pleased », he wrote that year, « to plaster his earth with violet mud. This is a novelty that is uninteresting and far too easy ». From these puerile reproaches let us retain only the following fact : Manet was at that moment far removed from the simple instructions which he had formerly received in the studio of Couture. He knew how to make use of local colour, but, through his contact with the Impressionists who owe him so much from the point of view of direct observation, he had learnt that an effect of shadow is not produced only by approaching local colour to black, but that it is the result of a decomposition of light within an area and on planes which can be perceived and rendered only in terms of cold colours.

Huysmans — and how many others! — were still among those critics for whom a painted work of art is only the illustration of literary thoughts; perhaps this race will never die out. Alphonse de Neuville, an excellent painter who had strayed into the anecdotal, wrote at once to Manet to tell him that from that time he had become worthy of decoration and that his approaching award would be considered as « a just reward for the sincerity and personal quality of your talent ».

The year 1881 was not less fruitfull of portraits and various other pictures. Manet passed the summer of this year at Versailles and, returning to Paris in the autumn, he immediately started, in his studio number 77 rue d'Amsterdam, to paint his picture *Le bar aux Folies-Bergère* (London, National Gallery), of which we have already spoken, and which was to be his last canvas of large dimensions. Manet in this work introduces his beautiful trenchant blacks with an effect of supreme charm among the brilliance of the table-cloth, the flowers and the large mirror which reflects, behind the young waitress, the bustle of the Music Hall.

But his illness was becoming worse. On the first of January in the year 1882, Antonin Proust, Minister of Fine Arts in the Gambetta Cabinet, ordered Manet to be awarded the Star of Chevalier of the Légion d'Honneur. Manet was becoming more and more ill. In the year 1882 he could scarcely paint anything but portraits, sometimes in oils, sometimes in pastels : several versions of Méry Laurent, with her little dog in her arms, or with her face shaded by a little veil, sometimes wearing a large hat, sometimes a toque of otter-fur, and the portrait of René Mazeroy, and that of Eliza, Méry Laurent's maid. He sent to the Salon his picture of *Le bar aux Folies-Bergère,* painted as has been said, at the end of the preceding year. His usual detractors, with Huysmans at their head, continued to assail him with their sarcasms.

He could scarcely walk any longer. He was hardly able to take more than a few steps in the garden of the house which he occupied during the summer at Rueil (formerly the house of Labiche), or to get far enough away to paint the exquisite landscapes showing the villa amid the verdant confusion of its surroundings. Soon it was impossible for him to move even a few yards. He continued however to paint still-life subjects, fruit and flowers. His friends, to whom he wrote letters full of good humour, illustrated with watercolours, gathered round him in turn. Too weak to hold a paint-brush all the time, he more and more often made use of pastels, a technique which had long been dear to him. It was then that so many young Parisian ladies, moved as much by sympathy as for snobbish reasons, came to pay him court. He never failed to find, among these fresh and elegant *Parisiennes* new sitters for his pastels, finished at a sitting, so rich in animation, but also, let it be confessed, rather accidental and not always, whatever may be said to the contrary, among his best work.

In the autumn, on his return to the studio at No. 77, rue d'Amsterdam, he still had the courage to form projects for a large canvas, *Le clairon* (« The trumpet »), for which he began a study on a canvas measuring 1 m. high by 0,81 m. wide. His friend, the painter Henri Dupray, was to serve as model; he possessed the uniform of an infantry trumpeter and a trumpet. Manet began his composition; it was destined in his imagination to represent him in the Salon of 1883. But his illness had made such progress that he could hold out no longer. That which had been taken for rheumatism was really the ill effects of an overworked nervous system : locomotor ataxy. Then, refusing to tolerate his disease and his diminishing physique any longer, and determined to free himself at all costs, Manet who was laid up with his left foot in a gangrenous condition, consented to an amputation. On April 30, 1883, at seven o' clock in the evening, he died.

Thus there passed away, at the age of only fifty one years, the man in whom the vast majority of his contemporaries saw only a careless amateur, a sort of practical joker. His work, none the less, amounted to 420 oil-paintings, 85 pastels, 114 watercolours, and quantities of engravings.

To each medium he brought something spontaneous, concise and perfect. By a sort of divination which belongs only to genius, he had laid the foundations for the language of plastic art most suited to succeeding generations and to the events which were to follow.

Less than a year after his death, a partial exhibition of his works was held in the Ecole des Beaux-Arts, to the catalogue for which Emile Zola contributed a preface. Many of those who had most violently attacked him, now dared, as always happens, to show themselves and to pose as his defenders from the first.

The victory was won for him; but the storm which he had raised was far from being calmed. Official institutions were sulky and disconcerted in the face of a glory in which they had no part, imposed on the public without their intervention. An artistic opinion had been created, independent of official opinion, of more value to artists and soon to be more profitable.

Of this divorce between the State and painters, disdainful of the official stamp, was born a long misunderstanding which is only to-day being dispersed.

MANET'S LETTERS

To M. Martinet.

Monsieur Martinet,

You ask me the price of the picture in your gallery (the boy with a sword). I should like a thousand francs for it, but I shall leave it to your discretion to let it go at eight hundred francs.

I beg to remain, dear Sir, yours very truly,

EDOUARD MANET.

To Duret, 1865.

Paris, 13 Oct.

My dear Duret,

I should have written to you before to tell you how much I have enjoyed reading your articles on Spain, but I was still away from Paris when your missive reached me, because on my return from la Sarthe I was seized with the indisposition which overcame almost all Parisians just at that time and we had gone to spend some days with our friends in the country; I am quite well now and going to start work again. I have, however, already done *la plaza de Toros de Madrid* since my return; on your next visit to Paris, do not fail to come and see me, I should so much like to have your redoubtable and decisive judgment.

But I hope that your articles are going to be continued and that you are going to speak of Spain from the artistic point of view — (Ve-

lasquez, Goya, Greco to the rescue!) — send them to me of course.

I look forward very much to seeing you again and to discussing our Spanish adventures but I shall never admit, I warn you in advance, that we dined well at Toledo.

Yours ever,

ED. MANET.

To a Friend.

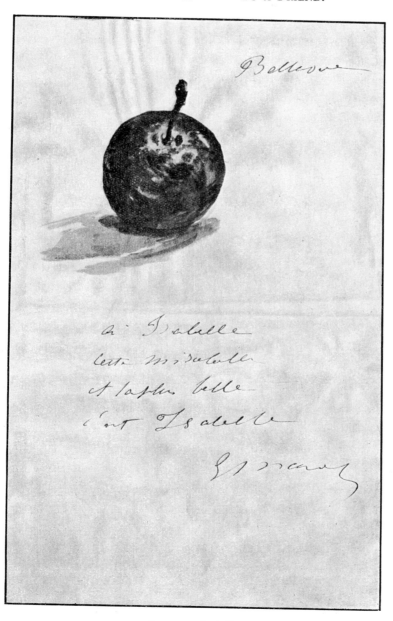

Letter to Isabelle.
(Musée du Louvre.)

4 Oct.

My dear friend,

Please send me Faure's address so that I can send him a proof of the guitarist.

Does he in fact like etchings and would he be pleased to have one? Because I am very miserly about a fine proof, at least for people who are indifferent to that kind of thing. All the same, I have every reason to believe and hope that our famous baritone is not among those.

Yours sincerely,

E. MANET.

To M. Cherman. 1866.

Monday, 15 Oct. 66.

Dear Monsieur Cherman,

I should like very much to show you some pictures I have in my studio and if you do not think me too presumptuous, I beg of you to name an afternoon when I may have the pleasure of receiving you.

Yours very sincerely,

ED. MANET.
rue Guyot, 81.

Letter to Isabelle.
(Musée du Louvre.)

To DURET.

18 March

My dear Duret, my frame-maker will call on you one of these days to measure the canvas (Study of a Young Girl) — they tell me there will be an exhibition on the 20th of May — he will take it away and I shall keep it till the sending in day so as not to bother you a little later on. Perhaps I shall also remove « The Balcony » from you and send it to London with « The Music Lesson » if I receive the letter of admission that I have asked for.

Yours sincerely,

EDOUARD MANET.

To DURET, 1871-5.

My dear Duret, I send you the little note you asked me for.

E. M.

« We learn that M. Manet has been refused permission to print a lithograph that he has just made representing the execution of Maximilian; we are surprised by this intervention of authority to impose an interdict on a purely artistic work ».

To DURET, 1871-75.

Saturday 27.

My dear Duret,

If among your acquaintances you should happen to have some collector in tow, I should be inclined just at the moment to make great reductions because I want some money.

Yours,   ED. MANET.

To M. BURTY, 1869.

Thursday, 18 Feb.

My dear Burty,

My Maximilian affair is getting complicated — the printer now refuses to give me back the stone and is asking my permission to efface it. Naturally, I am not only refusing to do this but also to take any of the steps which he is advising me to take to get the ban lifted and I sent him yesterday a legal summons. That's how things stand, but it seems to me an interesting point to know how it's going to turn out. One can't destroy the original design of a lithograph with the stone and everything by means of a legal injunction, so it seems to me, and at the very least, publication would be necessary, because that is what constitutes the offence.

I am sending you these new details in case it seemed opportune for you to mention them.

It's one of those questions which are important to thrash out for the sake of all artists who may find themselves in a similar plight.

Yours sincerely,   ED. MANET.

To J. DE LA ROCHENOIRE, 1870.

Saturday.

My dear la Rochenoire,

Our list has no chance of passing unless we make a bold stroke at the eleventh hour. My idea would be to burn our boats by getting the following notice published by the whole press and sending a copy individually to every artist whose work is coming up before the hanging committee :

« All those who are apprehensive of rejection should vote for the men whose names are appended below.

These men are believers in the right of every artist to show his work and to show it under the most favourable conditions. »

(The list of candidates follows here.)

If these idiots don't vote for us, we can't help it. It's good tactics, and after all we shall be standing up for the truth.

If one of the people on the list seems to be getting shaky, I've got an excellent recruit of *importance*. I'll tell you about it later on.

Yours ever,   MANET.

To Duret, 1870.

My dear Duret,
As it is very nice and rather rare to sell one's work to people who really like it, and as I know quite well that you appreciate the quality of the picture you are asking me for, I shall let it go to *you,* only I don't want anyone else to know the price, for the sum of 1200 frs. I shall be at the studio tomorrow at the time we said.
Ever yours sincerely,

ED. MANET.

I certainly shouldn't let a figure piece of that importance go to anyone, whoever it was, for less than 2500 francs. So if you agree to accept my price I should like it to be generally supposed that you didn't give less than 2000 for it.

To Duret.

Arcachon, 2 March.

My dear Duret,
I only got your letter this morning. We arrived here last night. I am writing this answer for the sake of conscience because I expect I shall see you during the day. If you had come with Eugène only, we could have put you up — we've got enough room for that.
See you soon,

ED. MANET.

To Duret, 1871.

Arcachon, Monday, 6 March.

My dear Duret,
It would be very kind if you could send me some money. I did hope to get some about now and so to avoid having to ask you for any before you produced it of your own accord. But I've got several things I must pay and I'm very hard up. We were sorry not to see you at Arcachon, you'd have been able to spend a nice day.
Yours ever,

EDOUARD MANET.

Chalet Servantie, 41, Avenue Ste. Marie,

To Duret, 1871.

Paris, 22 August.

My dear Duret,
I've received the cheque for 700 francs which you sent me from New York on the 9th of August; it has just arrived in time. You can imagine I must have been in great straits to have to hold a pistol to your head like that, but it's impossible to get any cash here at all — money is frightfully tight — the moratorium doesn't seem to have put the country's finances on their legs. I met Balleroy a few days ago, he proposed in committee to proclaim the republic, but the left wing absolutely opposed it on the plea that the Assembly is not constitutional. I think we shall before long be called upon to witness some manifesto or other from the General Staff.

Letter to Isabelle.
(Musée du Louvre.)

You're going to have a most interesting journey and there will be plenty to satisfy your spirit of curiosity and your love of art.

You mentioned Courbet — he behaved like a coward before the Council of War and is now unworthy of any interest.

Martinet announces an exhibition of pictures for the month of October; he knows quite a lot about the subject, but alas! *you* won't be there — one of the few really serious amateurs of our time. Degas, who is going ahead strongly and who before long will be a success, is in high hopes that some day soon he will figure in your gallery.

I had been told that you might be coming back soon, but the San Francisco address that you give me makes me think that you're going to carry out your original intention of going round the world. All right, good luck and a pleasant voyage. My best wishes to you from yours ever,

EDOUARD MANET.

TO MONTROSIER, 1874 (?).

Wednesday evening.

« Tout arrive »

My dear friend,

I am very grateful for your sympathy. I have had two pictures rejected — *le bal de l'Opéra,* and a landscape with figures. I really think these worthy painters are very badly brought up. However, if you were kind enough to help me a little, the damage would be reduced by half.

Kind regards,

EDOUARD MANET.

TO MONTROSIER, 1874.

Sunday, 25 May.

My dear friend,

I've not seen Mlle C. I shall be at home all day tomorrow till 5 o'clock and should like to have a talk with you.

Best wishes.

ED. MANET.

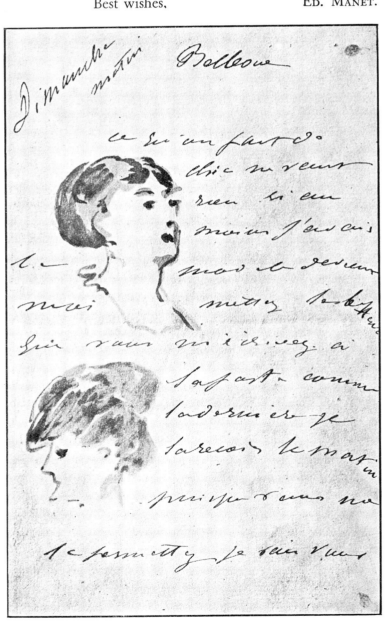

Letter to Isabelle.
(Musée du Louvre.)

TO MONTROSIER.

14 May.

My dear Montrosier,

I should like to revert to the question of the Punchinello. The proofs cost me so much that I see great difficulty in putting the sale price at 1 fr. 60. With the inclusion of the 25 signed and numbered proofs on loose Japanese paper which you could sell at 50 frs. to collectors, you ought not to do badly out of the deal. Please therefore arrange terms for me that I can accept. I've already taken to Lemercier's thirty sheets of various Japanese papers of the finest quality which I would give you.

I have been twice to Mlle Croisette's. Yesterday she was ill but no doubt we shall begin next week.

Yours sincerely,

ED. MANET.

10 May.

Dear Sir,

My final offer is this : I will sell you my Punchinello with all rights for the sum of 2000 frs. I would only ask you to let me have two or three proofs from it.

I beg you, my dear sir, to let me have your answer as soon as possible as this is a convenient moment for me to get this lithograph printed.

Yours faithfully,

ED. MANET.

TO MME CHARPENTIER,

Sunday.

Dear Madam,

The Punchinello is at your disposal, you can send to fetch it when you like.

Believe me, dear Madam, yours very truly,

ED. MANET.

Saturday, 10 October.

Sir,

I see on your invoice for the 18th of June an item for the effacement of seven stones for the Punchinello. *But I never gave you instructions to efface these stones.* If the effacement was not carried out, as I hope, I beg you to let me know and to put them on one side as I think I have found a buyer.

Yours truly,

ED. MANET.

TO THE PRINTER ?

Saturday.

Sir,

Please have my stone in readiness for *Monday;* I will send to fetch it.

You appear to be astonished at the way I have dealt

with you, but you no doubt forget that you refused to hand the stone over to me. I do not think that it was the fear of not being paid which inspired your course of conduct as you seem to imply in your last letter. The fact remains that, whether from one motive or another, you are asking me 75 frs. 50 for a stone which is worth 24 frs. I beg you to look into the matter.

I have had three trial proofs; I asked for four, but as I learn that one of them has been given to a M. R., I hope you will not put it down to me.

Yours truly,

E. MANET.

19 April.

My dear Master Engraver,

I recommend to you my friend Henri Guérard who has sent an etching after Holbein to the Salon; I think it is worthy of your approval.

I gather that it is you who are engraving the *bon Bock* for the Faure catalogue. I am delighted to hear it and I feel sure that your great skill will do justice to my work.

Yours sincerely,

EDOUARD MANET.

To MALLARMÉ.

My dear Mallarmé,

I sympathise with you and I think this is a season of sorrow. I too am very ill at ease myself to-day.

Yours sincerely,

E. MANET.

To THÉODORE DE BANVILLE.

« Tout arrive »

Saturday.

Dear Sir,

For the book of ballads entitled « *L'Assembleur de rimes,* » I want to do Banville at his table writing and smoking a cigarette; among the rising spirals of the smoke, I want to put small figures indicating the chief poems of the book.

If that suits you, I shall come and do a drawing at your house at the time and on the day you wish.

My sympathy and best wishes,

To THÉODORE DE BANVILLE.

« Tout arrive »

2 August.

Even at the cost of failing you as regards the etching for which I should so much have desired success, I am

grieved and ashamed but compelled to go away these next few days and it will be impossible for me to be ready before the month of September. I must therefore deny myself for the moment the honour and pleasure which I should have had in doing something for one of your books.

I remain, believe me, dear Sir, your friend and sympathiser,

E. MANET.

To ZACHARIE ASTRUC.

[5 June, 1880].
Bellevue, Monday.

You know, my dear Zacharie, the affection I feel for my old friends and the interest I feel in all their concerns, so that your letter and all the details you give me about your work and your hopes has given me great pleasure.

As you so rightly say, time is a great healer. I greatly

Letter to Isabelle.
(Musée du Louvre.)

23

Letter to Isabelle.
(Musée du Louvre.)

rely on it myself. I am living like a lizard in the sun, when there is any, and as much as possible in the open air; but certainly the country has no charms for those who are obliged to live there.

Proust is coming; he knows what store I set by your intelligence and your rare gifts. A recommendation won't get you a job on a paper. It's a shop, you know, where they take the goods which are likely to please the clientèle. Exercise your charm on him; you have a golden tongue.

came to dine yesterday at Bellevue; he is the personification of hope, he deserves to succeed, he has all the necessary qualifications; he began by getting his first Paris fashion design done by a Belgian. When will peoples' eyes be opened? Well, see you soon, my dear fellow, good luck and good health, which is after all the most valuable thing of all.

ED. MANET.

Bellevue,
41, route des Gardes.

TO DURET.

Bellevue.

Apparently I am the one who is wrong, but I didn't judge Zola's article from the personal point of view, and I thought I discovered too much eclecticism in it. We do so much need support in face of and against everyone, that a little radicalism would have done no harm, it seems to me. I await your verdict and I hope you will throw my first letter into the fire. I have received a letter on this subject from someone in whose opinion I have great confidence and who regrets that this article has not had more publicity. I am waiting for a line from you, my dear Duret, and I remain, believe me, your devoted friend,

ED. MANET.

MANET AND HIS CRITICS

« All artistic Paris, including the Ecole des Batignolles, as the Institut disdainfully puts it, is at the Hôtel Drouot. The sale room is in a ferment. The apostles of *plein air* pour forth the floods of their enthusiasm over the public. »

« There is going to be a change of opinion », they loudly proclaim. « Just as in the case of Courbet, he will be bought by the State. The absence of Manet leaves a gap in the Louvre. »

« The moment is a solemn one. It is no longer merely a question of praise and blame. The judgment we are awaiting is to come no longer from the Critic but from the Market; and it is often the Market that has the last word on the subject of a painter's reputation. »

. . . .

Are the Americans going to turn up to-day? Have the collectors been waiting to feel the public pulse before risking their money and their reputation? These and many more are the things we should like to know.

Purchases by faithful admirers have won the first round for Manet. All well and good. But what we should like to see him to do for the sake of himself, his friends and his school is to win the second round with the backing of the Americans, the collectors and the public galleries. »

. . . .

What points will be scored on the results of this sale by the naturalists, the impressionists and the intensionists?

The Louvre has made no purchases. Was it wrong? That is a problem I must ask my readers to solve. They know the answer; I do not commit myself. »

PAUL ENDEL
(*Le Figaro,* Febr. 4 and 5, 1884).

« I was there a whole hour and I watched with considerable uneasiness this horde of friends, enthusiasts and gamblers, keenly bidding against each other, not only for works in which Manet's gifts were triumphantly apparent, but also for things completely lacking in interest either from a speculative or an artistic point of view.

Pastel sketches, half obliterated by mouldering in the studio, fetched what were, comparatively speaking, fancy prices.

Goodness knows, I was devoted to Edouard Manet, but . . . .

The secret of these high prices is not to be looked for in the devotion of friends or in family influence. The truth of the matter is that there is a whole class of small collectors who are banking on the same rise of price in Manet as has already taken place, for instance, in Millet. A Millet pastel which the great man himself sold for a thousand francs is worth the same number of louis to-day.

How tempting to buy a Manet for four hundred francs and sell it in the future for four hundred louis! Wasn't the « Angelus » bought for three thousand francs and isn't it to-day worth two hundred and fifty thousand? These are golden dreams, but they are doomed, I am afraid, to end as nightmares! Any idea of belittling Manet is unthinkable to one who has watched as I have his early struggles, to one who has stood up for him through thick and thin. But Good Lord! don't let us lose our heads. Manet's friends are the devil; a dozen of those worthies would have been enough to do for Raphael and Michel-Angelo together. »

ALBERT WOLFF
(*Le Figaro,* Febr. 6, 1884).

« Caramba! Here is a *guitarero* who does not come off the stage of the Opéra-Comique, and who wouldn't look at all well in lithograph on the cover of a drawing-room ballad; but Velazquez would have greeted him with a friendly wink, and Goya would have asked him for a light for his *papelito*. With what a gusto he bawls his song and thrums his guitar! One can almost hear him at it... There is a great deal of talent in this figure; it is of life size, directly painted with a bold brush and the colour rings extremely true. »

THÉOPHILE GAUTIER
(*Le Moniteur Universel,* July 5, 1861).

« M. Manet, with instinctive bravado, has entered the domain of the impossible. But we absolutely decline to allow him to take us with him. In his large female portraits, all form disappears; this is particularly true of his *Chanteuse* (« Singer »). Here, with an oddity which profoundly disturbs us, the eyebrows have renounced their horizontal position to place themselves vertically on either side of the nose, like two dark commas. The whole thing simply becomes a shattering discord between tones of chalky white and tones of black; the effect is cadaverous, hard and morbid. »

PAUL MANTZ
(*La Gazette des Beaux-Arts,* 1863).

« *Lola de Valence* is celebrated in the following quatrain by Charles Baudelaire, which was hissed and abused as much as the picture itself :
« Entre tant de beautés que partout on peut voir,
» Je comprends bien, amis, que le désir balance,
» Mais on voit scintiller dans Lola de Valence
» Le charme inattendu d'un bijou rose et noir. »
(Between the varied charms that beauty can disclose,
My friends, I know too well desire can hardly choose;
But Lola de Valence can sparkle with the hues
Of some unheard of gem of sable and of rose.)

« I hold no brief for these lines, but for me personally they have the great merit of being a summing up in rhyme of the whole personality of the artist. It is perfectly true; *Lola de Valence* is a gem of sable and of rose. The painter's method here consists of patches of colour and his fair Spaniard is painted broadly and in vivid contrasts. »

EMILE ZOLA
(*Revue du XIXᵉ Siècle,* Jan. 1, 1867).

« But *is* this drawing ? *Is* this painting ? M. Manet, in attempting to be clear and forceful, only succeeds in being hard. The curious thing is, his hardness is only equalled by his woolliness. I can see clothes, but I fail to see the anatomical construction which underlies them and explains their conformations. I see whiskers apparently represented by two strips of black cloth gummed on to the cheeks. What more can I see ? This : a complete absence of conviction and sincerity on the part of the artist. »

CASTAGNARY
(*Salon,* 1863).

« The artist who, next to Mr. Whistler, is arousing the most discussion at the *Salon des Refusés* is M. Manet, another painter's painter. M. Manet's three pictures seem a little like a provocation to the public; it is offended by the excessive vividnes of their colour. There are some astonishing draperies in these two Spanish figures (« Young man in the costume of a *Majo* » and « Young woman in the costume of an *Espada* » which we describe below); the black costume of the Majo and the heavy scarlet cloak which he carries on his arm... but under these brilliant costumes the characters themselves seem to be absent. The heads ought to have been painted in a different style from the draperies, with more expression and greater solidity. »

THÉOPHILE THORÉ
(Salon of 1863. The Outcasts).

« *Le Déjeuner sur l'herbe* is Manet's greatest picture, the one in which he realises the dream dear to all painters, namely, setting life-size figures in a landscape. We know the powerful way in which he overcame the inherent difficulties. In the picture there is some foliage, some tree-trunks and in the background a river in which a woman is bathing in a shift; in the foreground are seated two young men opposite a second woman who has just emerged from the water and is drying her bare skin in the open air. This naked woman scandalised the public; she was the only thing in the picture they had eyes for. Good Heavens! how indecent! A woman without a stitch of clothing with two men fully dressed. Such a thing had never been seen. »

EMILE ZOLA
(*Revue du XIXᵉ Siècle,* Jan. 1, 1867).

« We have now come with a certain feeling of distaste to the strange pictures of M. Manet. To discuss them is a matter of some delicacy, but nevertheless we cannot pass them over in silence... in the eyes of many, it would be quite enough to pass them by with a smile; but that would be a mistake. We cannot afford to ignore M. Manet; he has a school, he has admirers; even fanatical admirers; his influence is more extensive than is supposed. M. Manet has this distinction, that he is a danger.

The danger is over now. From any point of view the *Olympia* is incomprehensible, even if we take it for that which it actually is, a wretched model lying at full-length on a sheet. The flesh tones are dirty, the modelling non-existent. Shadows are indicated by strokes of greater or less width executed in boot-polish. What are we to say of the negress bringing a bunch of flowers wrapped up in paper and of the black cat which leaves the mark of its muddy paws on the bed? Even the ugliness we could excuse if it were truthful, carefully observed or relieved by some splendid effect of colour. Even the ugliest woman has bones, muscles, a skin and some sort of colouring. Here there is nothing, we are sorry to say, except the desire to attract atention at all costs. »

THÉOPHILE GAUTIER
(*Le Moniteur Universel,* 24 June 1865).

« A truce to M. Manet! Ridicule has done justice to his pictures... But his painting which makes the critics and the public howl in unison is not that of a man lacking in temperament. M. Manet, I think, is of the number of those who could paint if they liked. »

EDMOND ABOUT
(*Le Petit Journal,* 27 June 1865).

« I should say that the grotesque side of the works exhibited by M. Manet was due to two causes : first of all, an almost childish ignorance of the first principles of drawing, then an almost inconceivable propensity for vulgarity...

He succeeds in provoking almost scandalous laughter among the visitors to the *Salon* who flock in front of the cockeyed individual (if the expression may be excused) whom he calls *Olympia.* »

ERNEST CHESNEAU
(*Le Constitutionnel,* 16 May 1865).

« There are also some paintings by M. Manet... Let us pass them by. One of our great foreign artists said to me on seeing these pictures : « Look what French painting has come to! » « You are mistaken », I replied, leading him up to *Les Faneuses* of Jules Breton. « That is what it has come to! »

M. DE THÉMINES
(*La Patrie,* 18 May 1865).

« *Olympia* reclining on her white sheets forms a large white mass against the dark background; in the dark background are to be seen the head of the negress who brings a bouquet, and the famous cat which has so much amused the public. At first sight, therefore, we can only distinguish two tones in this picture, two violent tones each contrasting with the other. Otherwise, details are indistinguishable. Look at the girl's head; the lips are two thin lines of pink, the eyes are reduced to a few black marks. Now look at the bunch of flowers, and look at it closely, please : patches of pink, patches of blue, patches of green. Everything is simplified, and if you want to reconstruct the reality you'll have to step back several paces. Then a curious thing happens : everything falls into its right place. The head of Olympia stands out against the background in strong relief, the bunch of flowers becomes a marvel of brilliance and freshness. »

EMILE ZOLA
(*Edouard Manet,* 1867).

La Femme au Perroquet.
« When in a painting there is neither composition, drama nor poetry, the execution must be perfect and this is not the case. I am told that this young woman was painted from a model with a fine head, a pretty and intelligent expression, and abundant tresses of the richest Venetian tint that a colourist could desire... The head we are shown is without doubt an unflattering likeness. The features are common and badly drawn and over them is spread an earthy colour which does not at all give the complexion of a young woman's fair skin. The light which should gleam and sparkle in the hair is dimmed and dull. The dress, of an unreal and muddy pink, does not reveal the form which it covers. »

THÉOPHILE GAUTIER
(*Le Moniteur Universel,* 11 May 1868).

« I roundly assert that the verdict of the jury in office this year is prejudiced. One whole aspect of the French art of our time has been arbitrarily withheld from us.... I don't deny it; I proclaim myself the champion of reality. I say quietly but firmly that I intend to admire M. Manet, that I care little for all M. Cabanel's powder and patchouli and that I prefer the pungent and healthy savours of Nature herself... We may laugh at M. Manet, but our sons will go into ecstasies over his pictures. »

EMILE ZOLA (signing *Claude*)
(*L'Evénement,* May, 1866. *My Salon*).

« I intend to-day to hold out the hand of sympathy to the artist who has been turned out of the Salon by a section of his colleagues. Even if my whole-hearted praise of him were not inspired by a great admiration of his talent, I should still have this incentive for it, that he has been forced into the position of a pariah as a grotesque and unpopular painter.

Before discussing those works which are there for all to see in the full light of their blatant mediocrity, I am making a point of devoting as much space as possible to an artist not considered worthy to hold a place among the fifteen hundred or two thousand incompetents who have been accepted with open arms.

.   .   .   .

« M. Manet's place in the Louvre is already marked out for him, like that of M. Courbet. »

EMILE ZOLA (signing *Claude*)
(*L'Evénement.* May 7, 1866. *My Salon*).

« M. Manet, through sheer incompetence, does not finish what he does, and he must credit the spectator with a generous dose of good will to add mentally what is lacking in his paintings.

Let us say at once that however bad the wo pictures rejected by the jury may be, the judges who have already admitted so many entries of Manet's should, for the sake of consistency, still admit him to-day We picture the famous *Olympia,* which made a whole genration rock with laughter, leaning up against the wall of the studio; well, between that picture and the works we see to-day, it must be admitted that the artist has made advances which the jury, to a certain extent, might have taken into consideration. All the same, it would have been more logical to refuse M. Manet's productions from the very first; he would thus have been spared the annoyance of getting on to the wrong track and he would have been able to take up some quite different

profession from painting for which he was possibly not adapted by Nature.

When after fifteen years of work a man arrives at the meagre results we see to-day, it must be agreed that it hardly seems to have been worth his while. »

EMILE PORCHERON
(*Le Soleil,* April 20, 1876).

« Being unable to see those funny little men they make out of gingerbread, I went instead to see M. Manet's two rejected pictures... The Jury has just done him the good turn of rejecting his two entries, thus reinforcing his popularity in the artistic world of the cafés. But could these two pictures of his not have graced the exhibition of his friends and brothers in arms, the impressionists? Why stand aloof? What added lustre the presence of M. Manet would have lent to that artistic coterie of cunning dogs who proudly entitle themselves impressionists and keep the flag flying as best they can till the day when they have at last learnt how to draw and wield a brush, if ever that day comes!

» Ah! Here are the two rejected pictures... « Horrible, most horrible! » as Shakespeare says. I recommend to the attention of spectators the lady, her child and the garden. What forms, what colours, what complexions!... The trees are flesh colour, the face resembles the dress, the washing hung out to dry has the solidity of the lady's body and the body has the flimsiness and unsubstantiality of the washing.

» Let us now turn to the portrait of M. Desboutins. Hail, my brave fellow! I don't know you personally, but France is in need of heroes! All Hail!... »

BERNARDILLE
(*Le Français,* April 21, 1876).

« How many nameless monstrosities must have been submitted to the jury in order finally to induce them to accept the *Portrait of M. Faure in the role of Hamlet* by M. Manet? It seems to me that the number of them must have been appalling, for M. Manet has never fallen as low as here. In the last few years he has exhibited a number of sufficiently farcical and ridiculous things, *La femme dans un parc* (Lady in a park), *à Argenteuil* (sic), for instance, but he has never offered anything so completely devoid of all quality as the picture which figures in the Salon to-day.

If I had not been assured that M. Faure had posed thirty-six or thirty-eight times for this portrait, I should have supposed that M. Manet had taken for his model one of those badly proportioned wooden puppets from a marionette theatre, whose limbs are dislocated, twisted, or badly fitted on... But enough. When criticism is confronted with work of this sort, its highest duty is to preserve an absolute silence. »

EMILE CARDON
(*Le Soleil,* May 3, 1877).

« M. Manet has had two pictures accepted this year. One called *Dans la serre* (In the Conservatory), represents a lady sitting on a green garden seat listening to the conversation of a gentleman who is leaning over the back of the seat. On all sides are tall plants, on the left some red flowers. The lady, who looks a little awkward and has a dreamy expression, is wearing a dress which looks as if it had been painted with big strokes at top speed — go and look at it, it is a superb piece of execution; the man is bare-headed, the light playing on his forehead, glancing here and there and falling on his hand which is done in a few strokes and is holding a cigar. In this position, absorbed in conversation, the figure is really a fine one; it is sparkling and alive. There is a free movement of air, the figures stand out splendidly against the mass of green which surrounds them. We have here a modern work of great attractions, a battle fought and won against the stereotyped representations of a sunlight which is never really seen in Nature. »

J.-K. HUYSMANS
(*L'Art Moderne,* 1879).

« The year is decidedly a bad one for now it is M. Manet's turn to go to pieces. Like a raw wine which is a little rough but has an unusual and pronounced flavour, this artist's painting used to be appetising and heady. Alas! it is now a sophisticated wine, coloured with aniline dye, despoiled of all its natural tannin, all its natural bouquet.

About his *Perthuiset* kneeling down and pointing his gun out into the room where he is apparently just sighting some suitable quarry with a yellowish and stuffed-looking lion lying behind him, really I don't know what to say. The pose of this whiskered sportsman who looks as if he were shooting rabbits in the woods of Cucufa is childish, and the picture is not superior in execution to the wretched daubs which hang round it. To distinguish himself from these, M. Manet has thought fit to render the ground in tones of mauve which is an uninteresting form of novelty and much too easy.

I am very much cast down at being obliged to pass this harsh judgment on M. Manet, but in view of the absolute sincerity which I have tried to maintain in this series of articles on the Salon, I have made it a matter of conscience to avoid falsehood and not to conceal from partisan motives my opinion on the work of this artist in the exhibition. »

J.-K. HUYSMANS
(*L'Art Moderne,* 1881).

« It is not possible to be more of a barmaid than the creature whom the artist has installed behind her marble slab loaded with fruit and bottles. But it is not in this that we see the essential merit of the work. That merit consists in the accurate perception of the things themselves, their colouring, their luminous vibration, their look of quivering insubstantiality, of fleeting rapidity. In this lies the triumph of M. Manet. He does not immobilise forms, as M. Béraud does in similar subjects; he surprises them in their actual mobility... It is an entirely new conception in art, very personal, very arresting, a direct conquest by the artist of the world of external phenomena, the fruits of which will not be lost to the future. »

ERNEST CHESNEAU
(*L'Annuaire illustré des Beaux-Arts,* 1882).

THE WORKS

« LE BON BOCK »
Photo Hyperion.

SELF PORTRAIT OF THE ARTIST
Photo Druet.

PORTRAIT OF HENRI ROCHEFORT
Photo Durand-Ruel.

PORTRAIT OF ANTONIN PROUST
Photo Durand-Ruel.

PORTRAIT OF RUBINI
Photo Druet.

THE ABSINTHE DRINKER
Photo Bulloz.

THE ARTIST (PORTRAIT OF MARCELLIN DESBOUTINS
Photo Durand-Ruel.

PORTRAIT OF GEORGE MOORE
Photo Durand-Ruel.

PORTRAIT OF EMILE ZOLA
Photo Hyperion.

PORTRAIT OF M. MAUREAU
Photo Bernheim Jeune.

THE LAWYER
Photo Bernheim Jeune.

THE PHILOSOPHER
Photo Durand-Ruel.

THE BEGGAR
Photo Durand-Ruel.

THE READER
Photo Durand-Ruel

PORTRAIT OF CAROLUS DURAN
Photo Durand-Ruel.

LOLA DE VALENCE
Photo Durand-Ruel.

PORTRAIT OF M. AND Mme AUGUSTE MANET
Photo Hyperion.

AT THE PRADO
Photo Hyperion.

A SPANISH WOMAN
Photo Hyperion.

PORTRAIT OF BERTHE MORISOT
Photo Bernheim Jeune.

THE WOMAN IN BLACK WITH A FAN
Photo Floury.

PORTRAIT OF BERTHE MORISOT
Photo Hyperion.

BERTHE MORISOT WITH A BUNCH OF VIOLETS
Photo Durand-Ruel.

A WOMAN SEATED
Photo Druet.

PORTRAIT OF MERY LAURENT
Photo Hyperion.

HALF-LENGTH PORTRAIT OF A WOMAN
Photo Durand-Ruel.

MISS C. CAMPBELL
Photo Durand-Ruel.

PORTRAIT OF MADEMOISELLE LATHUILE
Photo Durand-Ruel.

HEAD OF A PARISIENNE
Photo Durand-Ruel.

PORTRAIT OF MADAME MANET
Photo Durand-Ruel.

THE AMAZON (THE WOMAN WITH A HAT)
Photo Durand-Ruel.

STUDY OF A WOMAN
Photo Durand-Ruel.

PORTRAIT OF IRMA BLUMER
Photo Hyperion.

YOUNG GIRL SEATED ON A BENCH
Photo Durand-Ruel.

SPRING (PORTRAIT OF JEANNE DEMARSY)
Photo Durand-Ruel.

THE MILLINER
Photo Durand-Ruel.

PORTRAIT OF « TRONQUETTE »
Photo Durand-Ruel.

REPOSE
Photo Durand-Ruel.

EVA GONZALÈS
Photo Durand-Ruel.

PORTRAIT OF MADAME AUG. MANET
Photo Hyperion.

PORTRAIT OF A WOMAN IN A GARDEN
Photo Hyperion.

THE SULTANA
Photo Durand-Ruel.

A WOMAN WITH A PARROT
Photo Durand-Ruel.

YOUNG GIRL
Photo Durand-Ruel.

HEAD OF AN OLD WOMAN
Photo Durand-Ruel,

THE STREET-SINGER
Photo Durand-Ruel.

THE LADY WITH THE GLOVES
Photo Druet.

PORTRAIT OF MADAME EMILE ZOLA
Photo Floury.

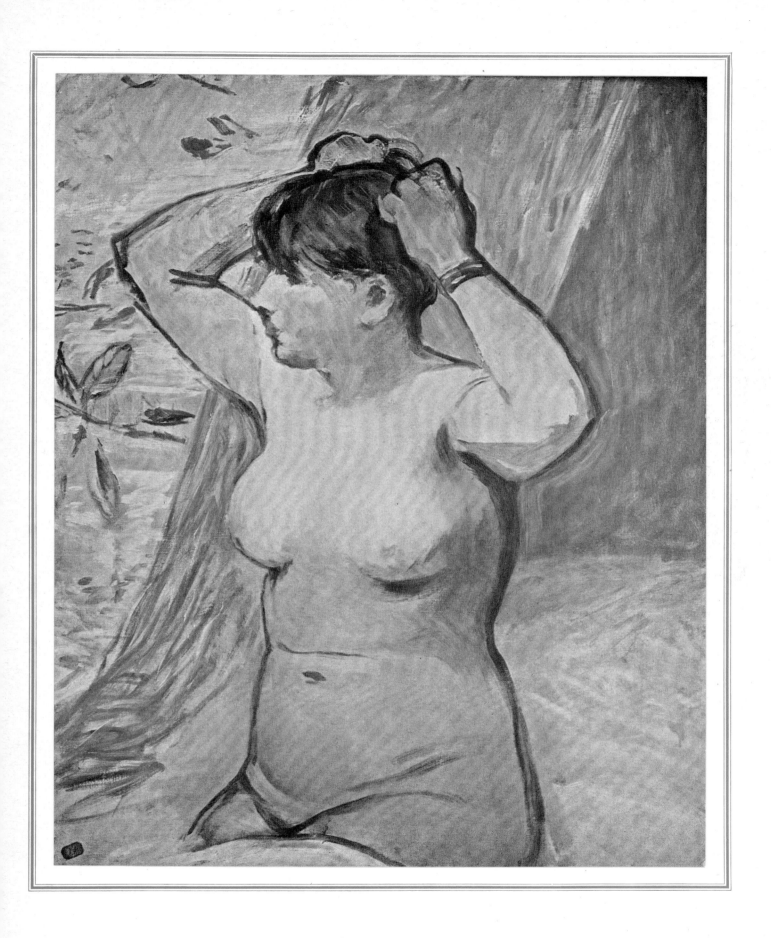

A STUDY OF THE NUDE
Photo Hyperion.

MADAME ED. MANET RECLINING ON A SOFA
Photo Floury.

THE LADY WITH FANS
Photo Floury.

YOUNG MAN PEELING A PEAR
Photo Hyperion.

BUBBLES
Photo Durand-Ruel.

LITTLE GIRL SEATED ON A BENCH
Photo Durand-Ruel.

HEAD OF A CHILD
Photo Durand-Ruel.

THE BOY WITH THE CHERRIES
Photo Durand-Ruel.

THE FIFER
Photo Hyperion.

THE SMOKER
Photo Durand-Ruel.

THE GUITAR-PLAYER
Photo Durand-Ruel.

91

A BAR AT THE FOLIES-BERGÈRE
Photo Durand-Ruel.

A BAR AT THE FOLIES-BERGÈRE
Photo Durand-Ruel.

AT THE CAFÉ
Photo Bulloz.

THE WAITRESS
Photo Durand-Ruel.

AT THE CAFÉ
Photo Durand-Ruel.

AT THE « PÈRE LATHUILE »
Photo Hypérion.

A CONCERT AT THE TUILERIES
Photo Durand-Ruel.

THE BALL AT THE OPERA
Photo Durand-Ruel.

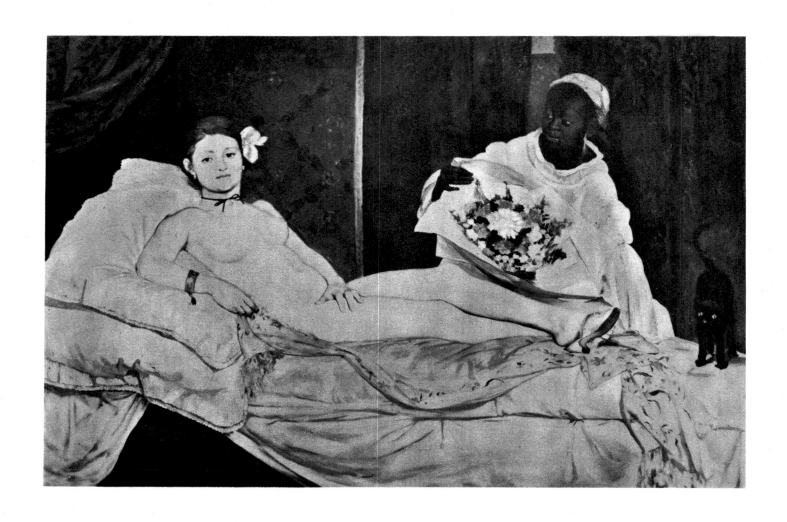

OLYMPIA
Photo Durand-Ruel.

THE PICNIC
Photo Durand-Ruel.

LUNCH AT THE STUDIO
Photo Durand-Ruel.

THE MANET'S HOUSE AT ARCACHON
Photo Durand-Ruel.

THE SKATING-RINK
Photo Durand-Ruel.

THE BALCONY
Photo Hyperion.

THE EXECUTION OF MAXIMILIAN
Photo Durand-Ruel.

THE EXECUTION OF MAXIMILIAN
Photo Durand-Ruel.

THE BARRICADE
Photo Hyperion.

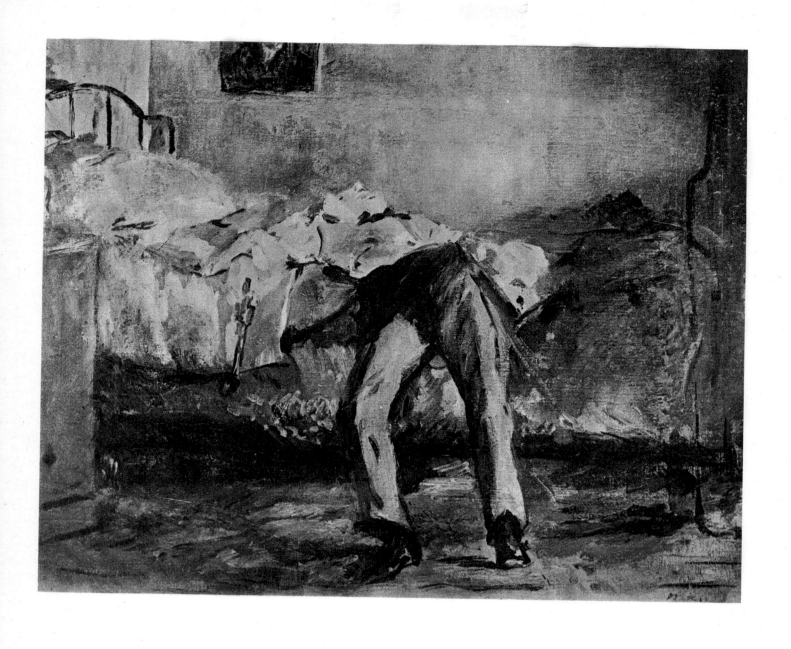

THE SUICIDE
Photo Durand-Ruel.

THE RAILWAY
Photo Durand-Ruel.

IN THE GARDEN
Photo Durand-Ruel.

WASHING-DAY
Photo Durand-Ruel.

ARGENTEUIL
Photo Hyperion.

THE ACTOR ROUVIÈRE
Photo Hyperion.

PUNCHINELLO
Photo Bernheim Jeune.

YOUNG MAN IN THE COSTUME OF A MAJO
Photo Durand-Ruel.

MATADOR SALUTING
Photo Durand-Ruel.

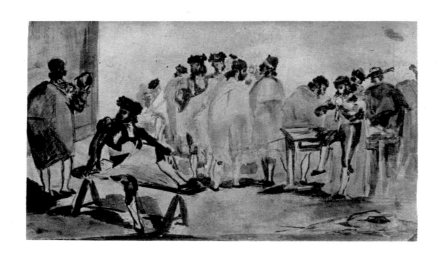

THE BULL-FIGHT
Photo Durand-Ruel.

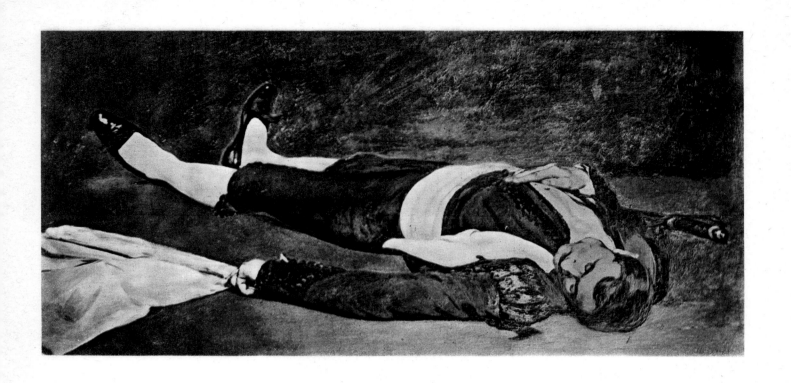

THE DEAD TORERO
Photo Durand-Ruel.

THE RACES AT LONGCHAMP

Photo Durand-Ruel.

THE RACES AT THE BOIS DE BOULOGNE
Photo Hyperion.

THE VIRGIN WITH THE RABBIT (AFTER TITIAN)
Photo Durand-Ruel.

THE OLD FIDDLER
Photo Durand-Ruel.

ROWERS
Photo Durand-Ruel.

MONET'S FLOATING STUDIO
Photo Durand-Ruel.

THE « RUE MOSNIER » DECKED WITH FLAGS
Photo Durand-Ruel.

ROAD MENDERS IN THE « RUE MOSNIER »
Photo Bulloz.

MANET'S GARDEN AT VERSAILLES
Photo Durand-Ruel.

LANDSCAPE
Photo Hyperion.

A STREET

Photo Druet.

THE WATERING-CAN
Photo Druet.

YOUNG GIRL IN THE GARDEN AT BELLEVUE
Photo Durand-Ruel.

A CORNER OF MANET'S GARDEN AT RUEIL
Photo Durand-Ruel.

RISING TIDE
Photo Knoedler.

LANDSCAPE
Photo Knoedler.

ON THE BEACH
Photo Durand-Ruel.

THE BEACH AT BOULOGNE
Photo Hyperion.

SEASCAPE
Photo Durand-Ruel.

THE FISHING-BOAT
Photo Durand-Ruel.

BOATS AT SEA
Photo Durand-Ruel.

ROUGH SEA
Photo Durand-Ruel.

THE PORT OF BORDEAUX
Photo Durand-Ruel.

ARGENTEUIL
Photo Bernheim Jeune.

NUDE STUDY OF A BRUNETTE
Photo Druet.

NUDE STUDY OF A BLONDE
Photo Hyperion.

THE GARTER
Photo Druet.

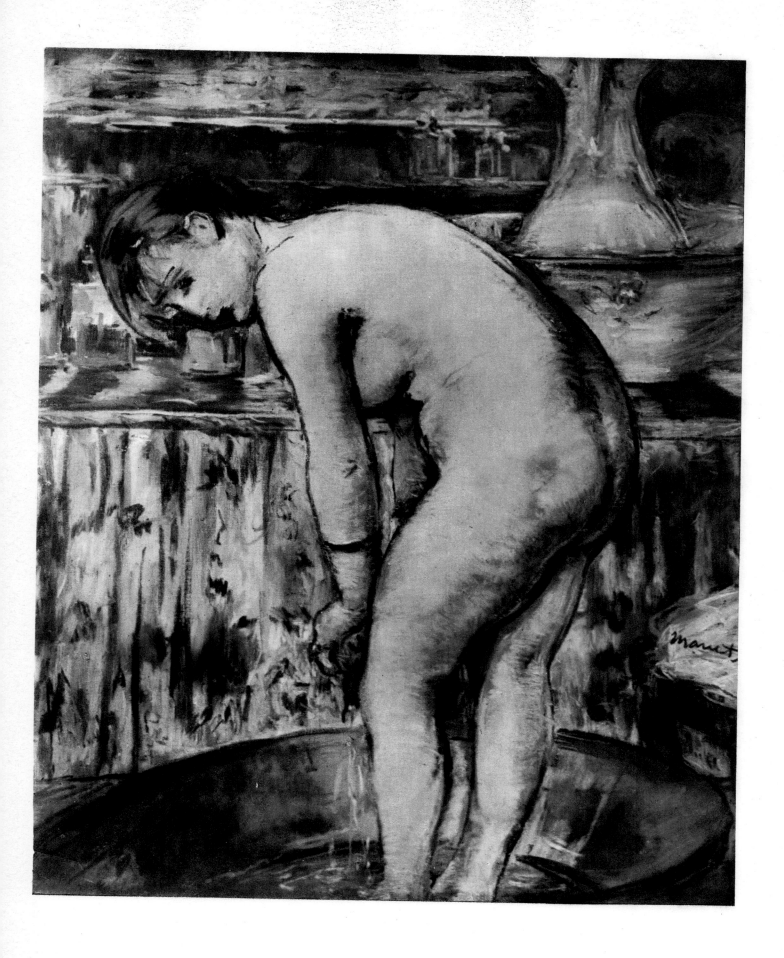

THE TUB
Photo Druet.

STUDY OF THE NUDE
Photo Durand-Ruel.

« NANA »
Photo Durand-Ruel.

THE SPANIEL
Photo Druet.

« FOLLETTE »
Photo Bernheim Jeune.

LILAC AND ROSES
Photo Druet.

FLOWERS
Photo Hyperion.

THE RABBIT
Photo Durand-Ruel.

THE HARE
Photo Bernheim Jeune.

STILL LIFE
Photo Durand-Ruel.

THE « BRIOCHE »
Photo Durand-Ruel.

A BASKET OF FRUIT
Photo Durand-Ruel.

OYSTERS
Photo Bernheim Jeune.

THE CAT AND THE FLOWERS
Photo Hyperion.

DETAILED DESCRIPTION
OF THE PLATES
AND REPRODUCTIONS

DETAILED DESCRIPTION
OF THE PLATES AND REPRODUCTIONS

33. « LE BON BOCK ». 1873. Canvas, 94 by 83 cm. Carroll Tyson collection, Philadelphia. Photo Hyperion.

34. SELF PORTRAIT OF THE ARTIST. 1879. Canvas, 83 by 67 cm. Jacob Goldschmidt collection, Berlin. Photo Druet.

35. PORTRAIT OF HENRI ROCHEFORT. 1881. Canvas, 82 by 67 cm. Kunsthalle, Hamburg. Photo Durand-Ruel.

36. PORTRAIT OF ANTONIN PROUST. 1856. Canvas, 56 by 47 cm. P. Cassiser collection, Amsterdam. Photo Durand-Ruel.

37. PORTRAIT OF RUBINI. 1858-1860. Canvas, 61 by 50 cm. Formerly Pellerin collection, Photo Druet.

38. THE ABSINTHE DRINKER. 1868. Canvas, 130 by 99 cm. Museum of Copenhagen. Photo Bulloz.

39. THE ARTIST. (PORTRAIT OF MARCELLIN DESBOUTINS). 1875. Canvas, 192 by 128 cm. Arnhold collection, Berlin. Photo Durand-Ruel.

40. PORTRAIT OF GEORGE MOORE. 1879. Canvas, 55 by 46 cm. Metropolitan Museum, New York. Photo Durand-Ruel.

41. PORTRAIT OF EMILE ZOLA. 1868. Canvas, 190 by 110 cm. Musée du Louvre, Paris. Photo Hyperion.

42. PORTRAIT OF M. MAUREAU. 1878. Pastel, 56 by 46 cm. Georges Bernheim collection, Paris. Photo Bernheim Jeune.

43. THE LAWYER. 1879. Canvas, 79 by 64 cm. Erich Goeritz collection, Berlin. Photo Bernheim Jeune.

44. THE PHILOSOPHER. 1863-1865. Canvas, 185 by 110 cm. Eddy collection, Chicago. Photo Durand-Ruel.

45. THE BEGGAR. 1865. Canvas, 185 by 110 cm. Art Institute, Chicago. Photo Durand-Ruel.

46. THE READER. 1861-1864. Canvas, 100 by 81 cm. Museum of Fine Arts, St. Louis, U.S.A. Photo Durand-Ruel.

47. PORTRAIT OF CAROLUS DURAN. 1876. Canvas, 190 by 157 cm. J. B. Stang collection, Oslo. Photo Durand-Ruel.

48. LOLA DE VALENCE. 1862. Canvas, 123 by 92 cm. Musée du Louvre, (Camondo collection), Paris. Photo Durand-Ruel.

49. PORTRAIT OF M. AND Mme AUGUSTE MANET. 1860. Canvas, 110 by 90 cm. Ernest Rouart collection, Paris. Photo Hyperion.

50. AT THE PRADO. Circa 1869. Aqua-fortis, 22 by 15 cm. Claude Roger-Marx collection, Paris. Photo Hyperion.

51. A SPANISH WOMAN. 1868. Aqua-fortis, 16 by 10,5 cm. Claude Roger-Marx collection, Paris. Photo Hyperion.

52. PORTRAIT OF BERTHE MORISOT. 1873. Study, 62 by 50 cm. Private collection. Photo Bernheim Jeune.

53. THE WOMAN IN BLACK WITH A FAN. 1874. Canvas, 72 by 83 cm. M. Gerstenberg collection, Berlin. Photo Floury.

54. PORTRAIT OF BERTHE MORISOT. 1873. Lithograph, 22 by 16,5 cm. Claude Roger-Marx collection, Paris. Photo Hyperion.

55. BERTHE MORISOT WITH A BUNCH OF VIOLETS. 1872. Canvas, 55 by 38 cm. Ernest Rouart collection, Paris. Photo Durand-Ruel.

56. A WOMAN SEATED. Canvas. Private collection. Photo Druet.

57. PORTRAIT OF MERY LAURENT. 1882. Canvas, 73 by 51 cm. Musée des Beaux-Arts, Nancy. Photo Hyperion.

58. HALF-LENGTH PORTRAIT OF A WOMAN. 1882. Pastel, 55,5 by 46,5 cm. Formerly Georges Viau collection, Paris. Photo Durand-Ruel.

59. PORTRAIT OF MISS C. CAMPBELL. 1875. Canvas, 54 by 44 cm. Formerly Pellerin collection. Photo Durand-Ruel.

60. PORTRAIT OF MADEMOISELLE LATHUILE. 1879. Canvas, 60 by 49 cm. Musée de Lyon. Photo Durand-Ruel.

61. HEAD OF A PARISIENNE. 1881. Pastel, 55 by 46 cm. Mrs. Coburn's collection, Chicago. Photo Durand-Ruel.

62. PORTRAIT OF MADAME MANET. 1866. Canvas, 100 by 76 cm. Private collection. Photo Durand-Ruel.

63. THE AMAZON. (THE WOMAN WITH A HAT). 1877. Canvas, 55,5 by 46 cm. Formerly Pellerin collection. Photo Durand-Ruel.

64. STUDY OF A WOMAN. Canvas, 55 by 46 cm. Private collection. Photo Durand-Ruel.

65. PORTRAIT OF IRMA BLUMER. 1882. Pastel, 54 by 45 cm. Musée du Louvre (Camondo collection), Paris. Photo Hyperion.

66. YOUNG GIRL SEATED ON A BENCH. 1872? Pastel, 60 by 50 cm. Formerly Dedon collection. Photo Durand-Ruel.

67. SPRING (PORTRAIT OF JEANNE DEMARSY). 1881. Canvas, 74 by 51 cm. Metropolitan Museum, New York. Photo Durand-Ruel.

68. THE MILLINER. 1880-1883. Canvas, 85 by 74 cm. Formerly Pellerin collection. Photo Durand-Ruel.

69. PORTRAIT OF « TRONQUETTE ». Canvas. Private collection. Photo Durand-Ruel.

70. REPOSE. 1869. Canvas, 149 by 113 cm. G. Vanderbilt collection, New York. Photo Durand-Ruel.

71. EVA GONZALÈS. 1880. Canvas, 200 by 135 cm. Tate Gallery, London. Photo Durand-Ruel.

72. PORTRAIT OF MADAME AUG. MANET IN THE GARDEN AT BELLEVUE. 1880. Canvas, 82 by 65 cm. Ernest Rouart collection, Paris. Photo Hyperion.

73. PORTRAIT OF A WOMAN IN A GARDEN. Canvas, 150 by 115 cm. Ernest Rouart collection, Paris. Photo Hyperion.

74. THE SULTANA. 1876. Canvas, 95 by 74,5 cm. Silberberg collection, Breslau. Photo Durand-Ruel.

75. A WOMAN WITH A PARROT. 1866. Canvas, 185 by 132 cm. Metropolitan Museum, New York. Photo Durand-Ruel.

76. YOUNG GIRL. Canvas, 112 by 93 cm. Private collection. Photo Durand-Ruel.

77. HEAD OF AN OLD WOMAN. 1856. Canvas, 50 by 40 cm. Paul Cassirer collection, Berlin. Photo Durand-Ruel.

78. THE STREET-SINGER. 1862. Canvas, 174 by 118 cm. Montgomery Sears collection, Boston. Photo Durand-Ruel.

79. THE LADY WITH THE GLOVES. 1860. Canvas, 130 by 98 cm. J. E. Blanche collection, Paris. Photo Druet.

80. PORTRAIT OF MADAME EMILE ZOLA. 1878. Pastel, 44 by 52 cm. Musée du Louvre, Paris. Photo Floury.

81. A STUDY OF THE NUDE. Canvas, 57 by 48 cm. Ernest Rouart collection, Paris. Photo Hyperion.

82. MADAME ED. MANET RECLINING ON A SOFA. 1874. Pastel, 49 by 60 cm. Musée du Louvre, Paris. Photo Floury.

83. THE LADY WITH FANS. 1874. Canvas, 113 by 168 cm. Musée du Louvre, Paris. Photo Floury.

84. YOUNG MAN PEELING A PEAR. 1868-1869. Canvas, 85 by 71 cm. Nationalmuseum, Stockholm. Photo Hyperion.

85. BUBBLES. 1867. Canvas, 100 by 82 cm. Adolph Lewinsohn collection, New York. Photo Durand-Ruel.

86. LITTLE GIRL SEATED ON A BENCH. 1880. Canvas, 74 by 61 cm. Durand-Ruel collection. Photo Durand-Ruel.

87. HEAD OF A CHILD. 1856. Pastel, 37 by 30 cm. Private collection. Photo Durand-Ruel.

88. THE BOY WITH THE CHERRIES. 1858-1859. Canvas, 65 by 55 cm. Gulbenkian collection, Paris. Photo Durand-Ruel.

89. THE FIFER. 1866. Canvas, 160 by 98 cm. Musée du Louvre, Paris. Photo Hyperion.

90. THE SMOKER. 1866. Canvas, 100 by 81 cm. Whitney collection, New York. Photo Durand-Ruel.

91. THE GUITAR-PLAYER. 1860. Canvas, 146 by 115 cm. W. Ch. Osborn collection, New York. Photo Durand-Ruel.

92. A BAR AT THE FOLIES-BERGÈRE. 1881-1882. Canvas, 47 by 56 cm. Franz Koenigs collection, Haarlem. Photo Durand-Ruel.
    THE ABSINTHE DRINKER (after Brouwer). 1858-1859. Canvas, 41 by 32 cm. Ny Carlsberg Museum, Copenhagen. Photo Durand-Ruel.

93. A BAR AT THE FOLIES-BERGÈRE. 1881. Canvas, 96 by 130 cm. Tate Gallery, London. Photo Durand-Ruel.
    MARIE COLOMBIER. 1880. Pen-and-ink portrait, 53 by 34 cm. Formerly Pellerin collection. Photo Durand-Ruel.

94. AT THE CAFÉ. 1874. Canvas, 46 by 38 cm. Walters collection, Baltimore. Photo Bulloz.

95. THE WAITRESS. 1878. Canvas, 98 by 79 cm. Tate Gallery, (Courtauld Fund, 1924), London. Photo Durand-Ruel.

96. AT THE CAFÉ. 1878. Canvas, 77 by 83 cm. Gerstenberg collection, Berlin. Photo Durand-Ruel.

97. AT « PÈRE LATHUILE'S ». 1879. Canvas, 92 by 112 cm. Musée des Beaux-Arts, Tournai. Photo Hyperion.

98. A CONCERT AT THE TUILERIES. 1860-1862. Canvas, 76 by 118 cm. Tate Gallery, London. Photo Durand-Ruel.
    YOUNG WOMAN DRESSING HER HAIR. 1878. Pastel, 56 by 46 cm. Private collection. Photo Knoedler.

162

99. THE BALL AT THE OPERA. 1873-1874. Canvas, 60 by 73 cm. Mme O. Havemeyer's collection. Photo Durand-Ruel.
THE BALL AT THE OPERA. 1873. Drawing. Photo Durand-Ruel.

100. OLYMPIA. 1863. Canvas, 150 by 190 cm. Musée du Louvre, Paris. Photo Durand-Ruel.
A STUDY OF THE NUDE. Water-colour, 28,5 by 41 cm. Private collection. Photo Knoedler.

101. THE PICNIC. 1863. Canvas, 214 by 270 cm. Musée du Louvre, Paris. Photo Durand-Ruel.
SKETCH OF THE PICNIC. Courtauld collection, London. Photo Druet.

102. LUNCH AT THE STUDIO. 1868. Canvas, 120 by 153 cm. Neue Staatsgalerie, Munich. Photo Durand-Ruel.

103. THE MANETS' HOUSE AT ARCACHON. 1871. Canvas, 39 by 54 cm. Metropolitan Museum, (Havemeyer Bequest, 1929), New York. Photo Durand-Ruel.

104. THE SKATING-RINK. 1877. Canvas, 92,5 by 72 cm. H. Cassirer collection, Berlin. Photo Durand-Ruel.

105. THE BALCONY. 1868-1869. Canvas, 169 by 123 cm. Musée du Louvre, Paris. Photo Hyperion.

106. THE EXECUTION OF MAXIMILIAN. Circa 1868. Canvas, 245 by 300 cm. Kunsthalle, Mannheim. Photo Durand-Ruel.
THE TRIAL OF BAZAINE. Private collection. Photo Bernheim Jeune.

107. THE EXECUTION OF MAXIMILIAN. 1867. Canvas, 50 by 61 cm. Museum of Copenhagen. Photo Durand-Ruel.
THE TRIAL OF BAZAINE. Private collection. Photo Bernheim Jeune.

108. THE BARRICADE. 1871. Aqua-fortis, 37 by 41 cm. Claude Roger-Marx collection. Photo Hyperion.

109. THE SUICIDE. 1881. Canvas, 36 by 45 cm. The Baron Hatvany's collection, Budapest. Photo Durand-Ruel.

110. THE RAILWAY. 1873. Pastel, 180 by 215 cm. Metropolitan Museum, New York. Photo Durand-Ruel.

111. IN THE GARDEN. 1870. Canvas, 43 by 55 cm. J. Watson-Webb collection, New York. Photo Durand-Ruel.

112. WASHING-DAY. 1875. Canvas, 145 by 115 cm. Paul Cassirer collection, Amsterdam. Photo Durand-Ruel.

113. ARGENTEUIL. 1874. Canvas, 149 by 131 cm. Musée des Beaux-Arts, Tournai. Photo Hyperion.

114. THE ACTOR ROUVIÈRE. Aqua-fortis, 30 by 16 cf. Claude Roger-Marx collection. Photo Hyperion.

115. PUNCHINELLO. 1873. Canvas, 50 by 32 cm. Lecomte collection, Paris. Photo Bernheim Jeune.

116. YOUNG MAN IN THE COSTUME OF A MAJO. 1863. Canvas, 196 by 130 cm. Metropolitan Museum, New York. Photo Durand-Ruel.

117. MATADOR SALUTING. 1866. Canvas, 171 by 113 cm. Metropolitan Museum, New York. (Havemeyer Bequest, 1929). Photo Durand-Ruel.

118. THE BULL-FIGHT. 1866. Canvas, 90 by 110 cm. Goldschmidt-Rothschild collection, Berlin. Photo Durand-Ruel.
LA POSADA. 1863. Water-colour. Formerly M. Lathuile's collection. Photo Knoedler.

119. THE DEAD TORERO. 1864. Canvas, 75 by 153 cm. Joseph Widener collection, Lynnwood Hall, Elkins Park, Philadelphia. Photo Durand-Ruel.
BULL-FIGHTERS. (Fragment). 1864. Canvas, 48 by 108 cm. J. A. Dunn collection, London. Photo Knoedler.

120. THE RACES AT LONGCHAMP. 1864. Canvas, 43 by 83 cm. Art Institute of Chicago. Photo Durand-Ruel.

121. THE RACES AT THE BOIS DE BOULOGNE. 1872. Canvas, 73 by 93 cm. Paul Rosenberg collection, Paris. Photo Hyperion.

122. THE VIRGIN WITH THE RABBIT (after Titian). 1859. Canvas, 70 by 84 cm. Miss Louise Robinson's collection, New York. Photo Durand-Ruel.
THE BOY WITH A SHEEP. 1859. Canvas, 19 by 17 cm. Formerly Grinnel collection. Photo Bernheim Jeune.

123. THE OLD FIDDLER. 1861. Canvas, 188 by 248 cm. Chester-Dale collection, New York. Photo Durand-Ruel.
THE STROLLING FIDDLER. 1862. Drawing, 24 by 32 cm. Photo Durand-Ruel.

124. ROWERS. 1874. Canvas, 96 by 130 cm. Metropolitan Museum, (Havemeyer Bequest, 1929), New York. Photo Durand-Ruel.

125. MONET'S FLOATING STUDIO. 1874. Canvas, 82 by 101 cm. Neue Staatsgalerie, Munich. Photo Durand-Ruel.

126. THE « RUE MOSNIER » DECKED WITH FLAGS. 1878. Canvas, 65 by 81 cm. Hayashi collection, Japan. Photo Durand-Ruel.

127. ROAD-MENDERS IN THE « RUE MOSNIER ». 1878. Canvas, 63 by 79 cm. Paul Cassirer collection, Berlin. Photo Bulloz.

128. MANET'S GARDEN AT VERSAILLES. 1881. Canvas, 65 by 81 cm. Durand-Ruel collection. Photo Durand-Ruel.

129. LANDSCAPE. 1880. Canvas, 46 by 54 cm. Ernest Rouart collection, Paris. Photo Hyperion.

130. A STREET. 1871. Canvas, 40 by 24 cm. Bernheim Jeune collection. Photo Druet.

131. THE WATERING-CAN. 1880. Canvas, 97 by 60 cm. Private collection, Essen. Photo Druet.

132. YOUNG GIRL IN THE GARDEN AT BELLEVUE. 1880. Canvas, 92 by 70 cm. Ed. Arnhold collection, Berlin. Photo Durand-Ruel.

133. A CORNER OF MANET'S GARDEN AT RUEIL. 1882. Canvas, 82 by 66 cm. Private collection, Berlin. Photo Durand-Ruel.

134. BOATS LANDING. 1872. Canvas, 50 by 61 cm. Barnes Foundation, Merion, Pa. U.S.A. Photo Knoedler.

135. LANDSCAPE. Canvas, 27 by 40 cm. Private collection. Photo Knoedler.

136. ON THE BEACH. 1872. Canvas, 38 by 44 cm. Paul Guillaume collection, Paris. Photo Durand-Ruel.

137. THE BEACH AT BOULOGNE. 1869. Canvas, 32 by 65,5 cm. A. Morhange collection, Paris. Photo Hyperion.

138. SEASCAPE. Canvas, 81 by 100 cm. Durand-Ruel collection, New York. Photo Durand-Ruel.

139. THE FISHING-BOAT. 1873. Canvas, 65 by 81 cm. Franz von Mendelssohn collection, Berlin. Photo Durand-Ruel.

140. BOATS AT SEA. 1873. Canvas, 34 by 53 cm. Private collection, U.S.A. Photo Durand-Ruel.
RISING TIDE. 1873. Canvas, 46 by 56 cm. Durand-Ruel collection, Photo Durand-Ruel.

141. ROUGH SEA. 1873. Water-colour, 15 by 23 cm. J. B. Faure collection. Photo Durand-Ruel.
CALM SEA. 1873. Water-colour, 16 by 23 cm. J. B. Faure collection. Photo Durand-Ruel.

142. THE PORT OF BORDEAUX. 1871. Canvas, 66 by 100 cm. Mme Robert von Mendelssohn's collection, Berlin. Photo Durand-Ruel.

143. ARGENTEUIL. 1874. Canvas, 60 by 81 cm. Formerly M. Genty's collection. Photo Bernheim Jeune.

144. NUDE STUDY OF A BRUNETTE. 1872-1875. Canvas, 60 by 49 cm. Ernest Rouart collection, Paris. Photo Druet.

145. NUDE STUDY OF A BLONDE. 1875-1878. Canvas, 59 by 49 cm. Musée du Louvre, Paris. Photo Hyperion.

146. THE GARTER. Circa 1880. Pastel, 53 by 44 cm. Wilhelm Hansen collection, Copenhagen. Photo Druet.

147. THE TUB. 1878. Pastel, 54 by 45 cm. Bernheim Jeune collection. Photo Druet.

148. STUDY OF THE NUDE. 1878. Pastel, 56 by 46 cm. Mme Ed. Berend's collection. Photo Durand-Ruel.

149. « NANA ». 1877. Canvas, 154 by 115 cm. Kunsthalle, Hamburg. Photo Durand-Ruel.

150. THE SPANIEL. 1866. Canvas, 45 by 37 cm. Private collection, Berlin. Photo Druet.

151. « FOLLETTE ». 1882-1883. Private collection. Photo Bernheim Jeune.

152. LILAC AND ROSES. Canvas, 32,5 by 23,5 cm. Knoedler collection, Paris. Photo Druet.

153. FLOWERS. Canvas, 34 by 26 cm. Féral collection, Paris. Photo Hyperion.

154. THE RABBIT. 1866. Canvas, 62 by 48 cm. Mme Jacques Doucet's collection, Paris. Photo Durand-Ruel.

155. THE HARE. 1881. Canvas, 97 by 60 cm. M. Emmanuel Chabrier's collection. Photo Bernheim Jeune.

156. STILL LIFE. 1866. Canvas, 69 by 92 cm. Eugene Mayer collection, New York. Photo Durand-Ruel.

157. THE « BRIOCHE ». 1870. Canvas, 65,5 by 84,5 cm. Leonard Gow collection, Glasgow. Photo Durand-Ruel.

158. A BASKET OF FRUIT. Canvas, 38 by 45 cm. John Spaulding collection, U. S. A. Photo Durand-Ruel.
ALMONDS AND A PEACH. 1864. Canvas, 17 by 22 cm. Private collection, Scotland. Photo Durand-Ruel.

159. OYSTERS. 1861-1862. Canvas, 38 by 46 cm. Gallimard collection Photo Bernheim Jeune.
ROSES AND PETALS. 1882-1883. Canvas, 16 by 21 cm. Bernheim Jeune collection. Photo Bernheim Jeune.

160. THE CAT AND THE FLOWERS. 1870. Aqua-fortis, 17,5 by 13 cm. Claude Roger-Marx collection, Paris. Photo Hyperion.

BIBLIOGRAPHY

BIBLIOGRAPHY

A. TABARANT : *Manet*. Histoire catalographique, Paris, Montaigne, edit. 1931.

This exhaustive study, devoid of all literature, definitely weighs the work of Manet. There is probably nothing left to glean after it. The slightest circumstances which affected the life and works of the artist are there collected with a patience and piety before which the historian must bow.

It would be futile to write about Manet without referring to this work at every step, which we have done throughout our study.

ARTISTE (L') : *Manet*. Articles or remarks. 1861, New series, vol. XII, p. 7; 1863, I, p. 148, 170; 1864, I, p. 242; 1865, I, pp. 224 to 228; 1866, I, p. 216; 1868, II, p. 245, 412; 1869, III, p. 403; 1872, I, p. 272; 1873, March-July, pp. 282-283; 1877, I, p. 342; II, pp. 37-38; 1878, II, p. 69; 1879, I, p. 396; II, p. 7 and p. 87; 1880, I, pp. 353-356-452; II, pp. 30-32; 1881, pp. 319-321.

ART MODERNE (L') *(et quelques aspects de l'art ancien)* : With forty poems by Henri de Régnier and many texts of criticism. 2 vol. in-4°. (Vol. I) Bernheim Jeune, publishers.

ASTRUC (Zacharie) : *Le Salon intime*. Exhibition of the Boulevard des Italiens, Paris, 1860, in-18°.

ASTRUC (Zacharie) : *Le Salon*. Daily chronicle issued every evening during the two months of the Exhibition. Paris, Cadart, 1863. in-8°.

AUTOGRAPHE (L') : *Album de l'Autographe au Salon de 1865 et dans les ateliers*. 104 pages of original sketches; 430 drawings by 352 artists. Paris, 1865.

BABOU (Hippolyte) : *Les dissidents de l'Exposition : M. Edouard Manet*. (« Revue Libérale », vol. II, 1867).

BALLU (Roger) : *Le Salon de 1878*. Peintres et sculpteurs. Paris, A. Quantin, 1878, in-4°

BALLU (Roger) : *La Peinture au Salon de 1880*. Les peintres émus, les peintres habiles. Paris, 1880, in-4°.

BASHKIRTSEFF (Marie) : *Journal*. Charpentier, 2 vol. in-12, 1887.

BAZIRE (Edmond) : *Manet*, with illustrations from the originals and from engravings by Guérard, Paris, A. Quantin, in-8°, 1884.

BENEDITE (Léonce) : *La Peinture au XIXe siècle*. 1900. in-4°

BERTAUT (Jules) : *Les souvenirs d'Henri Gervex*. (« Revue de Paris », October 1923).

BIEZ (Jacques de) : *Edouard Manet*. Lecture delivered at the Salle des Capucines, January 22nd, 1884. With a portrait after Fantin-Latour. Librairie d'Art L. Baschet, 1884.

BLANCHE (Jacques-Emile) : *Propos de peinture. De David à Degas*. 1st. series. Preface by Marcel Proust. Paris, 1919, in-18°.

BLANCHE (Jacques-Emile) : *Manet*. With 40 plates. « Les Maîtres de l'Art Moderne » series. Rieder, 1924.

BOUYER (Raymond) : *L'Art novateur du plein air. L'influence de Manet* (In the « Revue d'Histoire Contemporaine », May 2nd., 1891.)

BURTY (Philippe) : *Maîtres et petits maîtres*. Paris, 1880, in-18°.

CASTAGNARY : *Salons* (1857-1879). With a preface by Eugene Spuller. 2 vol. in-12°. Charpentier, 1892.

CASTAGNARY : *Le bilan de l'année 1868*. Paris, Le Chevalier, 1869, in-18°.

CASTAGNARY : *Les Artistes au XIXe siècle*. Salon of 1861. (1st series) Librairie Nouvelle, in-folio with plates.

CASTAGNARY : *Salon de 1868*. 48 pp. in-folio with plates.

CATALOGUE of the works of art (paintings, sculptures, engravings, lithographs and architectural designs) rejected by the committee of 1863, and exhibited by decision of H. M. the Emperor at the Salon Annexe, Palais des Champs-Elysées, on May 15th, 1863. — Paris, « Les Beaux-Arts », Revue de l' « Art ancien et moderne ».

CATALOGUE of the paintings of M. Edouard Manet, exhibited at the Avenue de l'Alma in 1867. — Paris, Imprimerie Poupard-Davyl, 30, Rue du Bac.

CATALOGUE of the Exhibition of the works of Edouard Manet at the Ecole Nationale des Beaux-Arts. With a preface by Emile Zola. Paris, A. Quantin, January, 1884.

CATALOGUE Ausstellung Edouard Manet, February-March, 1928, Matthiesen Gallery, Berlin.

CATALOGUE Manet auction. Paintings, pastels, studies, drawings and engravings by Edouard Manet and belonging to the estate. Hôtel Drouot, halls 8 and 9, on Monday and Tuesday, February 4th and 5th, 1884, at two o'clock. — Paris, Imprimerie Pillet and Dumoulin, 5, rue des Grands-Augustins, in-8°, 32 pp.

CHAUVELIN (Marius) : *L'Art contemporain*. With an introduction by W. Bürger (Th. Thoré). Paris, 1873, in-8°.

CHESNEAU (Ernest) : *Salon de 1882*. (In the « Annuaire Illustré des Beaux-Arts », 1882).

CLARETIE (Jules) : *Peintres et sculpteurs contemporains*. Paris, Charpentier & Cie, publishers, in-12°, 1873.

CLARETIE (Jules) : *L'Art et les artistes contemporains*. With a foreword on the Salon of 1876. Paris, Charpentier, in-12°, 1876.

COLIN (P.) : *Manet*, in-8°. Floury Edition, Paris, 1932. (96 illustrations).

COLLECTION CHERAMY : Analytical catalogue, preceded by studies of the principal Masters in the collection, by J. Meier-Graefe and Erich Klossowski. 127 reproductions in heliotype and 2 in photo gravure. Munich, R. Piper, publisher, 1908, in-4°.

COLLECTION GANYMEDE   Fac-similes of the works of Manet. (Reproductions of the Cassirer collection). Paris, Crès, publisher.

COURRIER ARTISTIQUE : *(Beaux-Arts. Expositions)*. Issued on the 1st and 15th of every month, 26, boulevard des Italiens, Director, Louis Martinet. (June 1861, May 1864).

CROS (Charles) : *Le Fleuve*. Aqua-fortis engravings of Edouard Manet. Paris, Librairie de l'eau-forte, 1874, in-4°.

CROS (Charles) : *Revue du Monde Nouveau, littéraire, artistique, scientifique*. 1st year, Paris, 1874.

DESNOYERS (Fernand) : *La peinture en 1863* (Le Salon des Refusés). Paris, 1863, 139 pp.

DRUET (Album d'Art) : 24 photoprints of the works of Manet, with a note by Florent Fels. Paris, 1928.

DU CAMP (Maxime) : *Le Salon de 1861*. Paris, A. Bourdilliat, in-18°.

DU CAMP (Maxime) : *Le Salon de 1864*. Paris, J. Claye, in-8°. (Extract from the « Revue des Deux-Mondes », June 1st, 1864).

DU CAMP (Maxime) : *Le Salon de 1865*. Paris, J. Claye, in-8°. (Extract from the « Revue des Deux-Mondes », 1st June, 1865).

DU CAMP (Maxime) : *Les Beaux-Arts à l'Exposition Universelle et aux Salons de 1863, 1864, 1865, 1866, 1867*. Paris, Vve Renouard. 1867, in-18°.

DURANTY : *La Nouvelle Peinture*. A propos du groupe d'artistes qui exposent dans les galeries Durand-Ruel. Paris, Denty, in-8°, 1876.

DURANTY : *Le Pays des Arts*. Paris, Charpentier, in-18, 1881.

DURET (Théodore) : *Les peintres français en 1867*. Paris, E. Dentu, publisher.

DURET (Théodore) : *Critique d'avant-garde*. Paris, Charpentier, publisher, 1885.

DURET (Théodore) : *Histoire d'Edouard Manet et de son œuvre*. (With a catalogue of paintings and pastels). First edition, H. Floury, 1902. Three Bernheim-Jeune editions, 1919-1926.

DURET (Théodore) : *Histoire d'Edouard Manet et de son œuvre*. (With twelve illustrations). Charpentier et Fasquelle, publishers, in-12°, 1906.

DURET (Théodore) : *Edouard Manet, sein Leben und seine Kunst, aus dem französischen ins deutsch*. (Translated by Dr. E. Waldmann-Bremen.) Cassirer, Berlin, 1910.

DURET (Théodore) : *Manet and the French Impressionists*. (Translated by J. E. Crawford-Flitch). London, 1910.

DURET (Théodore) : *Manet. Notice sur les « Trente-cinq tableaux de la collection Pellerin »* (exhibited in 1910 at Messrs. Bernheim-Jeune Gallery). Album in-4° jésus, with 8 photogravures.

DURET (Théodore) : *Les portraits peints par Manet et refusés par leurs modèles*. (In the « Renaissance de l'Art, July 1918).

DURET (Théodore) : *Manet y España*. Tradduccion y prologo de Ventura Garcia y Calderon. Illustrado con 26 reproducciones. Bernheim Jeune, publishers, 1927.

ETIENNE (Louis) : *Le jury et les exposants. Salon des refusés*. Paris, 1863, in-8°.

EVANS (Dr. Thomas-W.) : *Le Second Empire*. Memoirs of Dr. Evans, translated by E. Philippi, Paris, 1910, in-8°. Plon, publisher, 1928.

FELS (Florent) : *Manet*. « Les Albums Druet » collection, published by the Librairie de France, in-8°. (24 reproductions).

FENEON (Félix) : *L'impressionnisme en 1886*. « La Vogue » edition.

FLAMENT (Albert) : *La Vie d'Edouard Manet*. « Les grandes existences » collection. Publ. by Plon. 1 vol. in-18°. 1928.

FONTAINAS (André) and VAUXCELLES (Louis) : *Histoire générale de l'Art français de la Révolution à nos jours.* (Vol. I, Peinture-gravure. Part IX.) Librairie de France.

FOURCAULD (Louis de) : *L'Evolution de la Peinture en France au XIXe siècle.* Paris, 1890, large 8º.

GAUTIER (Théophile) : *Abécédaire du Salon de 1861.* E. Dentu, publ. 1861.

GEOFFROY (Gustave) : *Edouard Manet.* (In « La Vie Artistique », third series. E. Dentu, publ. 1894, in-18º.

GLASER (Dr. Curt) : *Edouard Manet.* (Faksimiles nach Zeichnungen und Aquarellen mit einer Vorrede). R. Piper and Co., Munich, 1922.

GONSE (Louis) : *Les Beaux-Arts et les Arts décoratifs à l'Exposition de 1878. L'Art Moderne.* (2 vol. published under the direction of Louis Gonse).

GONSE (Louis) : *Manet.* « Gazette des Beaux-Arts ». 1884, p. 133 et seq.

GOSSELIN (Théodore) : *Histoire anecdotique des Salons de Peinture depuis 1873.* Paris, in-12º, 1881.

HOURTICQ (Louis) : *Manet* (L'Art de notre temps). Librairie Centrale des Beaux-Arts, Paris.

HOUSSAYE (Henry) : *Le Salon de 1877.* (In the « Revue des Deux Mondes », of the lst and 15th June.)

HOUSSAYE (Henry) : *Le Salon de 1882.* (« Revue des Deux Mondes », lst and 15th June).

HOUSSAYE (Henry) : *L'Art Français depuis dix ans.* Paris, 1883.

HUYSMANS (J.-K.) : *L'Art moderne.* Paris, Charpentier, publ. in-12, 1883.

JAMOT (Paul) : *Le Fifre et Victorine Meurend.* In the « Revue de l'Art Ancien et Moderne », 1927.

JAMOT (Paul) : *Manet, peintre de marines.* (Le combat du « Kear-sage » et de l' « Alabama »). In the « Gazette des Beaux-Arts », 1927.

JAMOT (Paul) : *La Peinture au Musée du Louvre.* (XIXth Century, part III). Published by the « Illustration », under the directon of M. Jean Guiffrey.

JOURNAL DES CURIEUX : The issue of March 10th, 1907, entirely devoted to Manet.

LAFENESTRE (Georges) : *L'Art vivant.* The painting and sculpture of the Salons from 1868 to 1877, Paris, 1881, in-18.

LAGRANGE (Léon) : *La peinture et la sculpture au Salon de 1861,* Paris, « Gazette des Beaux-Arts », in-4º, fig. and pl.

LARAN (Jean) and LE BAS (Georges) : *Manet.* Forty-eight notes, preceded by an introduction by Louis Hourticq. With 48 plates hors-texte. Librairie Centrale des Beaux-Arts, in-12º, 1912.

LECLERCQ : *Caractère de l'Ecole Française de peinture.* Paris, in-12º, 1881.

LECOMTE (G.) : *L'Art Impressionniste.* 1892.

MANET : *Lettres de Jeunesse (1848-1849). Voyage à Rio.* Paris, publ. by Louis Rouart et fils, in-4º. 1929.

MARCEL (Henry) : *La peinture française au XIXe siècle.* Paris, 1905.

MAUCLAIR (Camille) : *L'Impressionnisme. Son histoire, son esthé-tique, ses maîtres.* Paris, 1904, in-8º.

MAUCLAIR (Camille) : *Les Etats de la peinture française, de 1850 à 1920.* Paris, Collection Payot, 1921.

MEIER-GRAEFE (Julius) : *Manet und sein Kreis.* (Manet and his Circle). « Die Kunst » collection, vol. VII, in-16º, 66 pp. and 9 plates. Berlin, 1903.

MEIER-GRAEFE (Julius) : *Entwickelungsgeschichte der modernen Kunst.* 3 vol. in-4º, 1904.

MEIER-GRAEFE (Julius) *Impressionisten* (Guys, Manet, Van Gogh, Pissarro, Cézanne). With an introduction on the value of French art. R. Piper & Cº, Munich-Leipzig, 1907.

MEIER-GRAEFE (Julius) : *Edouard Manet. Mit 197 Abbildungen.* R. Piper & Cº, Munich, 1912.

MEYER (Rudolf Aldebert) : *Manet und Monet* (Die Kunst unserer Zeit). Munich, 1908.

MOORE (George) : *Confessions of a Young Man.* 1886. Edited and annotated by George Moore. 1904, Londo , in-16º.

MOORE (George) : *Confessions d'un jeune Anglais.* Paris. Stock, 1925, in-8º.

MOORE (George) : *Modern Painting.* London, 1912, in-16º.

MOORE (George) : *Erinnerungen an die Impressionisten.* (Reminis-cences of the Impressionists), published by Max Meyerfield, Berlin. B. Cassirer, 1907, in-8º, illustr. and pl.

MOORE (George) : *Memoirs of my Dead Life.* London, 1906, in-16º.

MOORE (George) : *Mémoires de ma vie morte.* Translated by Jean Aubry. Paris, B. Grasset, in-16º, 1922.

MOREAU-NELATON *Manet graveur et lithographe.* With an engra-ving and 125 reproductions. Paris, 1906, in-4º.

MOREAU-NELATON : *Manet raconté par lui-même.* 2 vols. in-4º, with 353 reproductions. Paris, publ. by Laurens, 1926.

NITTIS (Joseph de) : *Notes et souvenirs.* Paris, Librairies-Imprimeries Réunies, 1895.

PELADAN (Josephin) : *Le Procédé de Manet* (D'après l'Exposition de l'Ecole des Beaux-Arts). Booklet of 16 pages, with numerous repro-ductions after the artist. Paris, 1884.

PIVA (Vittorio) : *Edouard Manet* (Estratto dal « Emporium », vol. XXV, nº 149, maggio 1907).

PAULI (Gustave) : *Raffael und Manet.* (In « Monatsheften für Kunst-wissenschaft », January-February, 1908.)

PROUST (Antonin) : *Souvenirs sur Manet.* (In the « Revue Blanche », February-March-April 1897).

PROUST (Antonin) : *Edouard Manet.* Reminiscences published by A. Barthelemy. Paris, Henri Laurens, 1913, in-8º.

REY (Robert) : *Choix de 64 dessins de Manet.* Publ. by Braun, 1932.

ROSENTHAL (Léon) : *Manet, aquafortiste et lithographe.* Paris, Le Goupy, publisher, 1925, in-8º.

SAINTE-CROIX (Camille de) *Edouard Manet* (In « Portraits d'hier », nº 19, December 15th 1909.) Paris, publ. by H. Fabre.

SEAILLES (Gabriel) : *Edouard Manet.* (In the « Revue de Paris », February 1910).

SALON REALISTE (Le) : By Vast-Ricouard and Gros-Kost. Cover illustrated by Manet, May lst, 1880. Publ. by Paul Ollendorff.

SAVARUS (Pierre de) : *Dix années d'art.* Reminiscences of exhibitions. Paris, in-8º, 1879.

SEVERINI (Gino) : *Edouard Manet.* (« Valori Plastici » editions). Rome, 1924.

SOCIETE DE REPRODUCTION DE DESSINS DE MAITRES. First to fourth years, 1909-1912. Fifth year, 1913. Paris, in-fol.

TABARANT (A.) : *Lettres de Manet, écrites pendant le siège de Paris, 1871.* Mercure de France, 1935.

THIIS (Jens) : *Manet.* (Kunstmuseets aarskrift). Copenhagen, 1917.

THORE (Théophile). *Salons de W. Burger, de 1861 à 1868.* (With a preface by Thoré). Portrait of W. Burger by Flameng. Paris, 1870, 2 vol. in-12º.

TOURNEUX (Maurice) : *Bibliographie des critiques des Salons.*

TSCHUDI (Hugo von) : *Edouard Manet.* With 24 reproductions from Durand-Ruel photographs. Berlin, 1902, in-8º. Publ. by Bruno Cassirer.

UHDE : *Les Impressionnistes.* Phaïdon Editions. 104 reproductions in photogravure, 14 plates in colour.

VERON (Pierre) : *Le Panthéon de poche.* (Manet, p. 194). Paris, publ. by Degorce-Cadot, 1875.

VIE MODERNE (La) : Literary and artistic illustrated weekly. 1879-1880, Paris, 2 vol. in-folio.

WALDMANN (Emil) : *Edouard Manet.* Publ. by Paul Cassirer, Berlin, 1923.

WALDMANN (Emil) : *Edouard Manet, sein Leben und seine Kunst.* Publ. by Paul Cassirer, Berlin, 1910.

ZOLA (Emile) : *Mon salon.* Paris. 1866. Librairie Centrale, in-12º.

ZOLA (Emile) : *Mes haines.* Causeries littéraires et artistiques. 1866, in-12º.

ZOLA (Emile) : *Edouard Manet.* Biographical and critical study, with a portrait of Manet by Bracquemond and an engraving by Manet after « Olympia ». Paris, 1867, in-8º. (From the « Revue du XIXe siècle »).

CONTENTS

PRINTED IN BELGIUM.